THE EMOTIONAL INTELLIGENCE ADVANTAGE

TRANSFORM YOUR LIFE, RELATIONSHIPS, AND CAREER

THE GROWTH LEADER COLLECTION

KIMBERLY BURK CORDOVA

COPYRIGHT

CONTENTS

INTRODUCTION

I had a moment in a bustling coffee shop, one that shifted my entire understanding of emotional intelligence. I was on a business trip, sitting across from a colleague who was venting about a project delay. My instinct was to jump in and offer solutions, but as the steam from our lattes fogged up my glasses, I realized that the frustration wasn't really about the project at all; it was about feeling heard. In that instant, I understood something crucial: emotional intelligence is about genuine connection, which can inspire hope and motivate us to build better relationships.

What Emotional Intelligence Really Means

Emotional intelligence (EI) isn't just a trendy concept; it's the transformative ability to recognize, understand, and manage not only our emotions but also those of the people around us. In a world that moves faster every day, this skill has never been more essential. Whether you're navigating personal relationships or leading a team at work, emotional intelligence can help you make genuine connections and achieve meaningful success, inspiring hope and a sense of possibility for your growth.

This book is not just a guide; it's a companion on my own journey with EI. It's for anyone who's ever misread a partner's silence, felt disconnected in a team setting, or simply wanted to better understand themselves. Through personal stories, practical exercises, and the latest research, I aim to equip you with tools to transform your life and relationships, fostering a sense of connection and understanding that encourages your personal growth.

Why This Book is Different

You'll find no cookie-cutter solutions here. Emotional intelligence is complex, and one size does not fit all. What sets this book apart is its commitment to authenticity and practicality. Each chapter is packed with real-life examples, exercises, and insights that reflect the messy, beautiful reality of human emotions. This book is designed for professionals, leaders, and anyone seeking personal growth, offering adaptable strategies for diverse situations.

What You'll Learn

The book is divided into three parts:

1. **Understanding Emotional Intelligence** – We'll cover foundational concepts and dive into the science behind EI.
2. **Enhancing Interpersonal Relationships** – Discover how EI can transform your personal and professional connections.
3. **Applying EI in the Workplace** – Explore advanced applications for leadership, team dynamics, and navigating the complexities of a diverse, global workforce.

By the end of this journey, you'll have tools not just for personal growth but for reshaping how you interact with the world.

My Story with Emotional Intelligence

My path to understanding EI has been anything but straightforward. I've been a single parent juggling work and a toddler, a new leader in high-stakes roles, and a partner working to build a deep, fulfilling relationship. Through all these experiences, from the stumbles to the breakthroughs, I've come to see the impact of emotional intelligence on every part of my life.

This book is an invitation to join me on a journey of self-discovery and growth. Whether you're a professional, a leader, a friend, or a partner, I hope you'll find tools here that resonate with you. EI isn't just about improving how you relate to others; it's about becoming the best version of yourself. So, as you turn the pages, I invite you to embrace this journey. Let's transform our lives and relationships together.

ONE

UNDERSTANDING EMOTIONAL INTELLIGENCE

In the heart of a bustling metropolis, amidst the cacophony of honking cars and hurried footsteps, lies an unassuming coffee shop. This place, a microcosm of the city's diverse populace, serves as the backdrop for an observation fundamental to our understanding of human interaction. Here, amidst the clatter of cups and the murmur of conversations, one can witness the intricate dance of emotional intelligence (EI) in action. From the barista who remembers a regular's order with a smile to the delicate negotiation between two friends navigating a disagreement, EI is the unseen force facilitating these exchanges. This everyday scene underscores a profound realization: emotional intelligence, the ability to recognize, understand, manage, and utilize emotions effectively in oneself and others, is not just a supplementary skill but the bedrock of meaningful human interaction.

The Evolution of Emotional Intelligence: Beyond IQ

The initial fascination with intelligence, traditionally measured through the narrow lens of the Intelligence Quotient (IQ), dominated early discourse. Yet, as our understanding of the human psyche deepened, a glaring oversight became apparent. The IQ test, with its rigid focus on logical reasoning, memory, and linguistic prowess, conspicuously ignored a critical component of human capability: the emotional domain. The emotional domain refers to the realm of feelings, emotions, and their management, which plays a significant role in our daily interactions and decision-making. The story of EI's ascent from the periphery of psychological research to a central pillar of contemporary understanding is not just a tale of academic curiosity but a radical reimagining of what it means to be intelligent.

The turning point in this narrative emerged from the work of psychologists John D. Mayer and Peter Salovey, who, in the early 1990s, proposed a model of emotional intelligence that challenged the prevailing IQ paradigm. Their work suggested that the ability to monitor one's own and others' feelings, to discriminate among them, and to use this information to guide one's thinking and actions was a form of intelligence unto itself. This proposition, while initially met with skepticism, ignited a scholarly and public fascination with the concept of EI. This fascination was fueled by the increasing recognition of the role of emotions in our lives and the potential of emotional intelligence to enhance personal and professional success. This led to its widespread acceptance as a critical component of personal and professional success.

The recognition of emotional intelligence as a skill set beyond the traditional IQ measures marked a paradigm shift in our understanding of intelligence. No longer was success in life and relationships solely the domain of those who excelled in academic or technical fields. Emotional intelligence opened the door to a more inclusive and holistic view of human capability, recognizing the importance of empathy, self-regulation, motivation, and social skills as equal, if not superior, predictors of success. This shift not only democratized the concept of intelligence but also highlighted the malleability and learnability of emotional skills, empowering those seeking to improve their interpersonal relationships and professional trajectories with a sense of acceptance and value for their growth potential.

The repercussions of this shift are still unfolding in today's fast-evolving world. As automation and artificial intelligence assume a greater role in the professional sphere, the uniquely human skill of emotional intelligence becomes increasingly valuable. The ability to empathize, collaborate, and navigate complex social dynamics is now recognized as a critical determinant of success in a wide range of fields. For instance, in leadership, emotional intelligence can help in understanding and managing team dynamics, in customer service, it can aid in empathizing with and addressing customer concerns, and in negotiation, it can facilitate understanding the other party's perspective. The future implications of this recognition are profound, suggesting a world where emotional intelligence is not just an asset but a necessity, shaping education, corporate training, and personal development practices worldwide.

In this evolving landscape, the everyday scenarios we encounter, from the coffee shop to the corporate boardroom, underscore the universal applicability of emotional intelligence. The barista who greets you by name, the manager who navigates a team conflict with grace, and the friend who listens with empathy are all practitioners of this critical skill set. These seemingly mundane moments are the threads that weave the fabric of our social world. They highlight the transformative power of emotional intelligence, making us all part of a larger narrative of understanding and connection and paving the way for personal and professional success.

As we delve deeper into the intricacies of emotional intelligence, let us remember that this journey is not about discarding the old in favor of the new. Instead, it is about expanding our understanding of what it means to be intelligent and recognizing the value of the emotional domain in enriching our lives and relationships. The evolution of emotional intelligence, from a mere psychological theory to a widely accepted skill set, offers a compelling narrative of growth and possibility, inviting us to explore the depths of our own emotional capabilities and the potential they hold for transforming our world.

Emotional Intelligence Unpacked: Self-Awareness, Self-Regulation, Motivation, Empathy, and Social Skills

In the landscape of emotional intelligence, five pillars stand tall, each a testament to the complex interplay of cognitive and emotional faculties that define our interactions with the world and its inhabitants. This dynamic framework, woven from the fundamental elements of self-awareness, self-regulation, motivation, empathy, and social skills, encapsulates the foundational emotional skills essential to our interactions and personal growth. It shapes our journey through the diverse challenges and possibilities life presents.

Defining Components

At the core of emotional intelligence lies self-awareness, the keen perception of one's inner landscape: emotions, strengths, weaknesses, and drives. This introspective clarity serves as the foundation for the other elements of emotional intelligence. It is the mirror reflecting our true selves, enabling us to navigate our emotional seas with precision and care. Close on its heels is self-regulation, the ability to manage and direct our emotions in a way that is both healthy and productive. Like the rudder of a ship, it steers us through turbulent waters, ensuring that we remain on course even in the face of adversity.

Motivation, the third pillar, fuels our journey, driving us toward our goals with a fervor and focus. It is the wind in our sails, propelling us forward with a passion that is undeterred by obstacles or setbacks. Empathy, the ability to understand and share the feelings of another, acts as the guiding compass in our interactions with others. It allows us to navigate the complex social landscapes we encounter daily, fostering deep, meaningful connections. Finally, social skills, the ability to communicate, persuade, and lead effectively, equip us with the tools necessary to build and maintain these connections, ensuring that we thrive in our personal and professional lives.

Self-Awareness

Imagine standing at the edge of a serene lake, the surface a perfect mirror, unrippled and clear. As you gaze into this natural mirror, you see not just your reflection but a window into your soul, revealing the depths of your emotions, strengths, weaknesses, and drives. This metaphor encapsulates the essence of self-awareness in emotional intelligence. It is a profound understanding of one's emotional state at any given moment, coupled with insight into how these emotions influence thoughts and actions.

The pursuit of self-awareness is akin to peeling an onion, layer by layer, each stratum revealing more of our inner selves. It takes courage to confront not just the aspects of ourselves we celebrate, but also those we might prefer to hide away. This journey inward illuminates the patterns of thought and behavior that shape our interactions with the world, allowing us to understand the why behind our reactions and decisions. With this knowledge comes the power to change, to grow, and to navigate our emotional landscapes with greater ease and confidence.

Self-Regulation & Motivation

Self-regulation and motivation, though distinct, are symbiotic, each influencing the other's efficacy. Self-regulation, the mastery over one's emotional responses, demands a level of emotional agility that allows us to respond to life's vicissitudes with grace rather than react with impulsivity. It is the disciplined commander of our emotional army, ensuring that our responses are measured, appropriate, and aligned with our long-term goals and values.

Motivation, on the other hand, is the fire that ignites our drive to pursue these goals. It is not merely the ambition to achieve but the resilience to persevere in the face of setbacks and failures. This intrinsic motivation, fueled by a passion for our pursuits and a commitment to our values, sustains us through the inevitable challenges life presents.

Empathy & Social Skills

Empathy, the ability to understand and share the feelings of another, is the bridge that connects us to those around us. It is not merely a passive experience of another's emotions but an active engagement with their perspective, a stepping into their shoes to view the world through their eyes. This deep, empathetic connection fosters a sense of understanding and solidarity that transcends mere acquaintance, knitting the fabric of our relationships into a cohesive whole.

Complementing this empathetic understanding are social skills, the tools we employ to navigate the complex web of human relationships. These skills, ranging from effective communication and conflict resolution to leadership and persuasion, enable us to interact with others in a respectful, productive, and enriching way. They are the tangible expressions of our emotional intelligence, the means by which we build and sustain the bridges of empathy that connect us to the world.

In this intricate dance of emotional intelligence, each step, self-awareness, self-regulation, motivation, empathy, and social skills, builds upon the last, creating a harmonious movement that carries us through life. This dance is not one of solitude but a collective performance, shared with those we encounter along the way, each interaction an opportunity to practice and refine our emotional competencies. As we move through the world, engaging with its challenges and joys, the principles of emotional intelligence guide us, ensuring that our journey is not just successful but meaningful.

The Science Behind Emotional Intelligence: Neuroplasticity and You

Beneath the intricate dance of social interactions and the silent whispers of introspection lies a realm where the tangible meets the intangible, where the biological scaffolding of our brains shapes the ethereal qualities of emotional intelligence. In this confluence, the ancient, reptilian structures of our limbic system intertwine with the relatively nascent neocortex, orchestrating the symphony of emotions that guides our thoughts and actions. This intricate interplay, a testament to the marvels of evolution, reveals a profound truth: our capacity for emotional intelligence is deeply rooted in the very architecture of our brains.

At the heart of this biological underpinning is the limbic system, a complex set of structures often heralded as the seat of our emotions. Here, nestled within the folds of the brain, the amygdala acts as the vigilant sentinel, appraising threats and pleasures. At the same time, the hippocampus, with its vast repository of memories, informs our emotional responses based on past experiences. Yet, these primal responses, untempered by the higher faculties of reason, would lead us astray were it not for the moderating influence of the prefrontal cortex. This latter region, a masterpiece of the neocortex, serves as the executive, integrating emotional impulses with cognitive processes to foster the nuanced expression of emotional intelligence.

Equally fascinating is the role of neuroplasticity in sculpting our emotional landscape. Once believed to be a static entity, the brain is now understood as a dynamic organ capable of remarkable transformation throughout our lives. This plasticity, the brain's ability to rewire itself in response to experiences, underpins our capacity to develop and enhance emotional intelligence skills. Each encounter, whether fraught with tension or brimming with joy, becomes an opportunity for growth as neural pathways are forged and strengthened, embedding the lessons of emotional regulation, empathy, and social interaction deep within the fabric of our brains.

The convergence of neuroscience and psychology has illuminated this process, offering compelling evidence of the brain's adaptability. Studies using functional magnetic resonance imaging (fMRI) have revealed tangible changes in the brain as individuals engage in practices designed to boost emotional intelligence. These practices, ranging from mindfulness meditation to targeted cognitive-behavioral interventions, have been shown to enhance connectivity between the amygdala and prefrontal cortex, facilitating better emotional regulation. Similarly, training in empathy and social skills has been linked to increased activity in regions associated with social cognition and emotional resonance, underscoring the brain's responsiveness to intentional efforts to hone emotional skills.

Yet the implications of this science extend far beyond academia, offering practical insights that can revolutionize our approach to emotional intelligence. Understanding that our brains are not only the source of our emotions but also malleable, shaped through deliberate practice, we are empowered to take an active role in our emotional development. This knowledge dismantles the myth of emotional intelligence as an innate, unchangeable trait, replacing it with a vision of continuous growth and adaptation.

Armed with this understanding, we can cultivate emotional intelligence with both humility and determination, recognizing that while the path may be challenging, it is also replete with possibilities. Practices such as mindfulness, which trains the brain to observe emotions without attachment, and cognitive reframing, which challenges us to interpret situations in a new light, become tools not just for personal betterment but for neural transformation. These practices, grounded in the science of neuroplasticity, offer a roadmap for enhancing our emotional intelligence, one neural pathway at a time.

Navigating the intricate landscape of human emotions and relationships, the revelations from the science of emotional intelligence and neuroplasticity shine as guiding lights. They guide our journey toward becoming more empathetic, resilient, and skilled in social interactions. In recognizing the profound interconnection between the biological and the emotional, we are reminded of the power that lies within us to shape not only our brains but also our lives and those of those around us. This understanding, deeply rooted in science yet immeasurably enriched by the nuances of human experience, offers a compelling vision of what it means to be emotionally intelligent in a world that is constantly evolving.

Measuring Your Emotional Quotient (EQ): A Starting Point

In the realm of personal development, few endeavors are as revealing and transformative as the quest to quantify one's emotional intelligence. This pursuit, far from a mere academic exercise, serves as a mirror reflecting the contours of our emotional landscape, offering insights that are both profound and actionable. At the heart of this exploration lies the concept of the Emotional Quotient (EQ), a metric that endeavors to capture the essence of our emotional capabilities in a manner that is both comprehensible and quantifiable.

At its core, EQ signifies a transformative shift in how we perceive intelligence. It moves us beyond the conventional emphasis on cognitive skills, inviting us to appreciate the complex emotional abilities essential for meaningful human connections. It acknowledges that the ability to navigate the complexities of our inner emotional world and to engage effectively with others is not peripheral but central to our overall functioning. In this light, EQ emerges not as a static measure but as a dynamic indicator of our capacity for empathy, self-regulation, and social interaction. It offers a nuanced perspective on what it means to be truly intelligent.

The endeavor to assess one's EQ is facilitated by a diverse array of tools and methodologies, each designed to peel back the layers of our emotional self. From standardized assessments like the Mayer-Salovey-Caruso Emotional Intelligence Test (MSCEIT) to more introspective approaches such as self-report questionnaires like the Emotional Quotient Inventory (EQ-i), these tools offer a structured pathway to self-discovery. Yet, the act of measurement is only the beginning. The actual value of these assessments lies in their ability to catalyze introspection and growth, prompting us to confront the realities of our emotional competencies and deficiencies.

Interpreting the results of these assessments demands a delicate balance between objectivity and compassion. It requires us to stand as impartial observers of our own psyches, to confront our limitations without judgment, and to celebrate our strengths without complacency. This process, though at times uncomfortable, holds potential. It lays bare the areas that demand our attention and effort, whether it be cultivating greater empathy, enhancing our ability to regulate distressing emotions, or refining our social skills. In this light, the outcome of an EQ assessment is not a verdict but a roadmap guiding our journey towards emotional maturity.

Actionable steps mark the journey from assessment to improvement, each tailored to the unique contours of our emotional landscape. For those grappling with emotional regulation challenges, techniques grounded in mindfulness and cognitive-behavioral approaches offer a pathway to greater equilibrium. Practices such as focused breathing, meditation, and the conscious reframing of negative thought patterns not only soothe the turbulence of our emotional seas but also fortify our minds against future storms.

In the quest to enhance empathy, the deliberate practice of perspective-taking stands as a powerful tool. Engaging with diverse narratives, whether through literature, cinema, or direct interaction with others, expands our emotional repertoire, enabling us to inhabit others' worlds with authenticity and compassion. This practice, when coupled with active listening and the cultivation of curiosity about the lives of those around us, deepens our capacity for empathy, enriching our relationships and our understanding of the human condition.

For those seeking to elevate their social skills, the path forward is one of engagement and reflection. It involves not only engaging in social situations but also adopting a reflective stance towards them. Feedback from trusted peers, coupled with self-reflection on social encounters, offers invaluable insights into our communicative styles, revealing opportunities for enhancement. Techniques such as the deliberate use of open-ended questions, active listening, and the cultivation of non-verbal communication skills are practical steps towards more effective and fulfilling interactions.

In this nuanced exploration of emotional intelligence, the measurement of EQ emerges not as an end but as a means, a starting point on a journey towards self-understanding and growth. It challenges us to confront the complexities of our emotional selves, to embrace the vulnerability of self-discovery, and to engage in the deliberate practice of emotional skills. This process, though demanding, holds the promise of transformation, offering a pathway to a richer, more connected, and more fulfilling life.

In the midst of our busy lives, enhancing our emotional intelligence represents a profound shift, recognizing the value of our emotions as central to our human experience. It invites us to look beyond the surface, to delve into the depths of our emotional world, and to emerge with a deeper understanding of ourselves and our place in the human community. In this endeavor, the measurement of EQ serves not merely as a metric but as a mirror, reflecting not just who we are but who we might become.

The Myths of Emotional Intelligence: Debunking Common Misconceptions

In the realm of personal and professional development, few concepts have been as simultaneously embraced and misunderstood as emotional intelligence (EI). Emotional Intelligence (EI), a complex mosaic of abilities essential for navigating our interactions globally, has frequently been clouded by myths and misconceptions, veiling its authentic essence and possibilities. This section seeks to illuminate the reality of emotional intelligence by dispelling some of the most pervasive myths that surround it.

First among these misconceptions is the belief that emotional intelligence is an innate trait, fixed at birth and immutable throughout life. This view, rooted in a deterministic understanding of human capabilities, fails to account for the dynamic interplay between genetics and the environment that shapes our emotional landscape. In truth, emotional intelligence is far from static; it is a skill set that can be developed and enhanced through intentional practice and reflection. The science of neuroplasticity, which reveals the brain's capacity to change in response to experience, underscores this reality and offers a compelling rebuttal to the notion of EI as an unchangeable attribute. By engaging in practices that foster self-awareness, empathy, and emotional regulation, individuals can significantly alter their emotional intelligence, expanding their capacity for understanding and connection.

Another myth that has taken root in the discourse around emotional intelligence is its purported irrelevance to leadership roles. This belief, predicated on an outdated model of leadership that prioritizes assertiveness and decisiveness to the exclusion of all else, overlooks the profound impact that emotional intelligence has on leadership effectiveness. Leaders with high emotional intelligence not only manage their own emotions but also excel at understanding and influencing others' emotions. This ability to navigate the complex emotional dynamics of teams and organizations enhances communication, fosters collaboration, and facilitates conflict resolution, making emotional intelligence an indispensable tool for effective leadership. Far from being irrelevant, EI emerges as a critical determinant of leadership success, challenging the conventional wisdom that equates leadership with emotional detachment.

The conversation around emotional intelligence has also been marred by gender stereotypes that associate emotional intelligence predominantly with women, implicitly suggesting that men are somehow deficient in this area. This stereotype, grounded in traditional notions of gender roles, fails to recognize the universality of emotional intelligence across the gender spectrum. Emotional intelligence, encompassing skills such as empathy, self-regulation, and social adeptness, is not the province of any one gender but a human capability that can be developed by anyone, regardless of gender identity. By perpetuating this stereotype, we not only reinforce harmful gender norms but also deprive individuals of the opportunity to explore and enhance their emotional intelligence free from the constraints of societal expectations. The reality is that emotional intelligence transcends gender, offering a pathway to deeper understanding and connection for all individuals.

Finally, it is crucial to address the misconception of emotional intelligence as a panacea, a cure-all solution for personal and professional challenges. While the benefits of emotional intelligence are manifold, ranging from improved relationships to enhanced leadership capabilities, it is not a magical elixir that can resolve all problems. Emotional intelligence operates within the broader context of an individual's life and is influenced by factors such as personality, upbringing, and situational variables. Moreover, the practical application of emotional intelligence requires not only possessing these skills but also the wisdom to know when and how to use them appropriately. It is a valuable tool in our developmental arsenal, but like all tools, its efficacy depends on the skill and discernment of the user. Recognizing the limitations of emotional intelligence while appreciating its considerable value enables us to cultivate it with realistic expectations and a commitment to ongoing growth.

In dispelling these myths, we shed light on the true nature of emotional intelligence: a dynamic, learnable skill set that is critical to personal and professional success. By embracing the complexity and nuance of emotional intelligence, we open ourselves to profound transformation, moving beyond misconceptions to a deeper understanding of our emotional capabilities and their potential to enrich our lives and those around us.

Chapter Summary: Understanding Emotional Intelligence

Introduction to Emotional Intelligence (EI)

- Emotional intelligence (EI) is the ability to recognize, understand, manage, and use emotions effectively in oneself and others. It is illustrated through everyday scenarios, such as a barista remembering a customer's order or friends resolving a conflict. These moments reflect how EI is fundamental to meaningful human interactions.

The Evolution of Emotional Intelligence: Beyond IQ

- Historically, intelligence was primarily measured by IQ tests, which emphasized cognitive skills such as reasoning and memory. However, as psychology advanced, it became evident that IQ alone did not encompass the full range of human capabilities, notably emotional and social skills.
- Psychologists John D. Mayer and Peter Salovey introduced the concept of EI in the early 1990s, proposing it as a separate form of intelligence. This idea broadened the definition of intelligence to include skills such as empathy, self-regulation, and social awareness.
- Recognizing EI's importance marks a significant shift in understanding human potential, with applications now extending to fields like leadership, customer service, and team dynamics. In a world increasingly shaped by automation, EI is emerging as a critical skill set that machines can't replicate.

The Science Behind EI: Neurology and Neuroplasticity

- EI is rooted in brain regions such as the amygdala, which processes emotions, and the prefrontal cortex, which manages emotional responses. Neuroplasticity, or the brain's ability to rewire itself, enables growth in EI skills over time.

- Studies using functional MRI (fMRI) show that practices such as mindfulness can strengthen connections between the amygdala and the prefrontal cortex, enhancing emotional regulation and empathy.
- This understanding reveals that EI is not fixed but can be developed through intentional practice, such as cognitive reframing and mindfulness techniques. These practices reshape the brain's neural pathways, fostering greater emotional awareness and resilience.

The Five Pillars of Emotional Intelligence

1. **Self-Awareness**: Recognizing and understanding one's own emotions, strengths, and weaknesses. Self-awareness serves as the foundation for the other components of EI, promoting introspection and self-reflection.
2. **Self-Regulation**: The ability to manage emotions in a way that is healthy and productive. This skill is crucial for maintaining composure and responding thoughtfully to challenges.
3. **Motivation**: An internal drive to pursue goals with passion and persistence. Motivation in EI is about being intrinsically driven, fueled by personal values and a desire for growth.
4. **Empathy**: The capacity to understand and share the feelings of others. Empathy fosters deep connections and helps navigate complex social interactions.
5. **Social Skills**: Effective communication, conflict resolution, and leadership abilities. Social skills are essential for building and maintaining relationships and are the outward expressions of one's EI.

Measuring Emotional Intelligence: The Role of EQ

- Emotional Quotient (EQ) tests, such as the Mayer-Salovey-Caruso Emotional Intelligence Test (MSCEIT), offer a means to assess and understand EI levels. These assessments provide insights into personal strengths and areas for improvement.
- Interpreting EQ scores can serve as a roadmap for growth, emphasizing that EI skills can be nurtured over time through targeted exercises and self-reflection.

Debunking Myths About EI

- Common misconceptions about EI include the belief that it is an innate, unchangeable trait or that it is irrelevant in professional settings. However, neuroplasticity demonstrates that EI can be cultivated, and research highlights its relevance for effective leadership.
- Another myth suggests that EI is more aligned with women due to gender stereotypes, yet EI is a universal skill set applicable across the gender spectrum. Finally, while EI is beneficial, it is not a cure-all for personal and professional challenges; it requires wise application and complements other skills.

Conclusion

Emotional intelligence is a dynamic and learnable set of skills with profound implications for personal and professional success. As we continue to understand the science behind EI and its practical applications, we open ourselves to greater self-awareness, resilience, and deeper connections with others.

TWO

SELF-REFLECTION:
THE UNSEEN MIRROR

In an unremarkable moment on a Tuesday afternoon, as sunlight lazily sifted through the window, casting long shadows across the room, the profound realization that self-awareness is akin to navigating a vast, uncharted ocean struck me. The tools of navigation, compass, map, and stars, are much like the techniques of self-reflection: indispensable yet often overlooked. Without them, sailing the turbulent seas of our emotions and thoughts becomes an aimless drift. This chapter introduces the compass and charts of self-reflection, guiding us through the introspective process that unveils the depths of our emotional intelligence.

The Importance of Self-Reflection

Self-reflection, the cornerstone of emotional intelligence, is like the first step in a garden where stones are yet to be laid, but the path is clear. It's the process of turning the gaze inward, not in judgment but in curiosity, to understand the motives that drive us and the emotions that sway us. This inward gaze is pivotal; it illuminates the patterns of our thoughts and feelings, much like how a lighthouse reveals the hidden dangers to sailors in the dark. Through self-reflection, we gain clarity not only about our emotional state but also about how our state influences those around us. This clarity empowers us, putting us firmly in the driver's seat of our emotional intelligence journey.

Reflection Techniques - Meditation and Journaling: Tools for Introspection

Two of the most effective tools in the self-reflection toolbox are meditation and journaling. Meditation, in its essence, invites silence, creating a space for the mind's chatter to subside and for more profound thoughts and feelings to surface. It teaches the mind to observe without attachment and to notice emotions as they arise without being swept away by their current. In contrast, journaling offers a canvas for these emotions and thoughts, a place where they can be articulated, examined, and understood. Together, these practices foster a habit of introspection, strengthening the muscles of self-awareness with each session.

For meditation, begin with five minutes a day, focusing on the breath, noticing the thoughts that arise, and gently guiding the focus back to the breath when the mind wanders. For journaling, dedicate a few minutes each night to write about the day's emotional landscape; what triggered strong emotions, how you reacted, and what thoughts accompanied these feelings.

Feedback Loops - The Role of Feedback in Enhancing Self-Awareness

Feedback serves as a mirror, reflecting how others perceive our emotional and social presence. It closes the loop in self-awareness, offering an outside perspective that can confirm or challenge our self-perceptions. This 'feedback loop' is a continuous process of seeking, receiving, and incorporating feedback, especially in professional settings or from close relationships. It transforms feedback from mere commentary into valuable insights, enhancing our self-awareness and emotional intelligence. The key lies in asking specific questions that go beyond generalities, such as, "Can you give an example of when I handled a situation well emotionally?" or "How do you feel I react under stress?"

Case Studies - Real-Life Applications of Self-Reflection

Understanding and managing emotional triggers can bring a profound sense of relief, knowing that we have the power to navigate our emotional responses. This is a significant part of the transformative power of self-reflection.

Another case involved a university professor who, through feedback, discovered her lectures were perceived as disengaged. She adopted journaling to reflect on her passion for teaching and meditation to be more present. This led to a revitalization of her teaching method, making her classes more interactive and engaging, as noted in subsequent student feedback.

These cases underscore the transformative power of self-reflection, highlighting how integrating feedback can lead to profound personal growth and enhanced emotional intelligence. They serve as inspiring examples of the potential for personal transformation inherent in the practice of self-reflection.

Emotional Journaling: Tracking Your Emotional Landscape

Within the quiet confines of a journal's pages lies a potent tool for self-discovery, a sanctuary where the tumultuous waves of our emotions find solace and understanding. Emotional journaling, far from being a mere repository of daily events, serves as a reflective lens, magnifying the intricate patterns of our emotional responses and the triggers that elicit them. This practice, rooted in the tradition of introspection, offers a structured approach to navigating the complexities of our inner worlds, providing clarity amidst the chaos of unexamined feelings and thoughts.

Journaling Benefits

The act of putting pen to paper, or fingers to keys, to articulate the nuances of our emotional experiences offers myriad benefits, transcending the simple act of recording. This deliberate articulation forces a slowing down, a pause in the relentless pace of life, allowing for a meticulous examination of our emotional states. Through this examination, journaling acts as a conduit for the transformation of nebulous feelings into coherent narratives, lending voice to previously unexpressed emotions. The benefits of this practice are manifold, encompassing not only enhanced self-awareness but also a reduction in stress and anxiety, as the act of writing provides a means of processing and releasing pent-up emotions. Furthermore, journaling fosters a heightened sense of empathy towards oneself, encouraging a gentle, non-judgmental approach to personal flaws and shortcomings. It also helps in improving memory, boosting mood, and enhancing problem-solving skills.

Getting Started

Embarking on the journey of emotional journaling requires little in the way of preparation but much in terms of commitment. The initial step is deceptively simple: choose a medium that resonates, be it a classic notebook or a digital app, and set aside a regular time each day for this practice. The absence of a rigid structure allows for creativity and personalization in approach. However, for those seeking guidance, prompts such as "Today, I felt ___ because ___" or "A situation that challenged me today was ___" can serve as starting points, gently nudging the mind towards introspection. The key is consistency, for it is through regular engagement with this practice that the more profound benefits of journaling are realized.

Pattern Recognition

As the journal fills with daily reflections, a complex picture begins to emerge, revealing recurring emotional responses and their triggers. This process uncovers patterns that might have stayed hidden, offering valuable insights into our habitual reactions. This 'Pattern Recognition' is a key aspect of emotional journaling. By identifying recurrent themes in our emotional reactions, be they anger at perceived slights or anxiety in anticipation of social gatherings, we gain insights into the underlying triggers that propel these responses. Such awareness is the first step in developing coping strategies, as it enables anticipating and mitigating emotional reactions in similar future scenarios. The key to successful pattern recognition lies in the regular review of journal entries, approaching them with a detective's eye for connections and recurring motifs.

Long-Term Growth

The consistent practice of emotional journaling offers not merely a snapshot of our emotional lives at a given moment but a longitudinal study of personal growth and evolution. Over time, the journal becomes a repository of victories and setbacks, a testament to the journey of emotional maturation. This archive of personal history serves not only as a reminder of the obstacles overcome but also as a motivator for continued growth, highlighting areas of emotional intelligence that have seen improvement and those that still require attention. Moreover, the act of journaling itself evolves, shifting from a tool for emotional regulation to a sophisticated instrument for self-reflection and empathy, facilitating deeper connections with oneself and, by extension, with others.

In the quietude of reflection, as we traverse the landscapes of our emotions through journaling, we engage in a dialogue with our inner selves. This dialogue, rich in insights and revelations, guides us towards a more nuanced understanding of our emotional beings. Through the meticulous tracking of our emotional responses and the triggers that elicit them, we develop not only a map of our emotional terrain but also the navigational skills necessary to traverse it with wisdom and grace. The practice of emotional journaling, therefore, stands as a cornerstone of emotional intelligence, a practice through which we chart the course of our personal and emotional growth.

The Power of Mindfulness in Cultivating Self-Awareness

Within the intricate weave of human consciousness, where thoughts and emotions intertwine in an elaborate ballet, mindfulness shines as a clear guiding light. This ancient practice, rooted in the wisdom of centuries, offers a path to navigate the internal landscape with a sense of presence and attentiveness, transforming mere observation into a profound understanding of the self. At its core, mindfulness is the deliberate act of attending to the present moment with an attitude of openness and curiosity, without the cloud of judgment or the distraction of past regrets and future anxieties. This quality of being fully immersed in the now, with a gentle yet focused awareness, holds the key to unlocking the depths of self-awareness, revealing the patterns and undercurrents that shape our emotional world.

Mindfulness Defined

To grasp the essence of mindfulness is to understand its role as the observer within, a silent witness to the ebb and flow of our inner experiences. It transcends mere passive awareness, embodying an active engagement with the present that cultivates a deep, nuanced understanding of our thoughts, feelings, and bodily sensations. This practice, far from a passive retreat into the self, is an exploration of the richness of the moment, a way to attune to the subtleties of our inner dialogue and emotional responses with an equanimity that enlightens and empowers.

Mindfulness Practices

For those standing at the threshold of this practice, the journey begins with simple, accessible techniques that usher in a state of mindful awareness. One foundational practice is conscious breathing, where the focus is on the breath as it flows in and out, a lifeline to the present that gently coaxes the mind away from its wanderings. This can be complemented by mindful observation, a practice in which one selects an object of focus, perhaps a leaf or a candle flame, and allows all attention to be absorbed by the details of its form, texture, and color, thereby training the mind in the art of focused awareness.

Another technique, the body scan, invites a sequential attention to different parts of the body, from the tips of the toes to the crown of the head, noting any sensations, tensions, or discomfort with a curious, non-judgmental stance. This not only enhances bodily awareness but also reveals the intricate connection between physical sensations and emotional states. Each of these practices, in its simplicity, opens a doorway to the profound, cultivating mindfulness that illuminates the landscape of the self.

Impact on Emotional Intelligence

The infusion of mindfulness into the fabric of our daily lives brings forth a transformative impact on emotional intelligence, sharpening the lens through which we view our emotional selves. At the heart of this transformation is an enhanced self-awareness, a clarity and depth of understanding that allows us to recognize and name our emotions with precision, discerning their nuances and origins with a discerning eye. This awareness extends beyond the self, improving our capacity to empathize with others. Mindfulness cultivates a sensitivity to the emotional states of those around us, enabling a more compassionate, attuned interaction.

Furthermore, mindfulness equips us with the tools to navigate our emotional seas with skill and grace, fostering resilience by enabling us to approach challenging emotions with a calm, centered presence. By training the mind to remain anchored in the present, mindfulness mitigates the tendency towards reactive, impulsive responses, paving the way for thoughtful, measured reactions that reflect mature emotional intelligence. This direct impact of mindfulness on the pillars of emotional intelligence, self-awareness, self-regulation, empathy, and social skills illuminates its value as a cornerstone of personal and relational growth.

Integrating Mindfulness

The true potency of mindfulness lies not in sporadic engagement but in its seamless integration into the rhythm of our lives. This integration begins with recognizing mindfulness as a practice not confined to moments of formal meditation but as an approach to life itself. Simple acts, such as savoring the flavors of a meal, listening intently to a piece of music, or fully engaging in a conversation, become opportunities to cultivate mindfulness, transforming mundane activities into exercises in presence and awareness.

Moreover, incorporating mindfulness into daily routines, perhaps through brief mindful breathing each morning or mindful pauses before responding in conversations, ensures that this practice becomes a sustained source of clarity and equanimity. It is in these moments, scattered like jewels throughout the day, that mindfulness weaves its subtle magic, gradually transforming our relationship with our emotions, with others, and with the world at large. This integration of mindfulness, a gentle yet profound infusion of awareness into the fabric of everyday life, stands as a testament to its transformative power, a reminder of the capacity within each of us to cultivate a rich, insightful understanding of the self through the simple act of being present.

Identifying Emotional Triggers: A Deep Dive

Within the labyrinthine paths of our inner landscapes lie hidden snares; emotional triggers, poised to spring forth unexpectedly, unraveling the fabric of our composure with startling ease. These triggers, deeply embedded within the psyche, serve as conduits to our most profound vulnerabilities and fears, evoking reactions that often perplex and dismay us in their intensity. To navigate this terrain with foresight and agility necessitates an intimate understanding of these concealed mechanisms; an exploration into the origins and nuances of our emotional triggers that is both enlightening and indispensable for the cultivation of self-awareness.

Emotional triggers, at their core, are intricate tapestries woven from the threads of past experiences, memories, and unresolved conflicts. They act as alarm systems, signaling a perceived threat to our emotional well-being, often rooted in past traumas or deeply held insecurities. The seemingly innocuous triggering event acts as a key, unlocking a floodgate of emotions that, to the untrained observer, might appear disproportionate to the cause. This dichotomy between stimulus and response lies at the heart of the trigger's power, underscoring the need to unravel these complex emotional responses to regain equilibrium and insight.

The process of identifying one's emotional triggers begins with meticulous observation and vigilance in responding to seemingly mundane interactions and events. It demands acute sensitivity to the nuances of emotional shifts and an attunement to the subtle cues that herald the onset of a triggered response. This observational vigil can be augmented by reflective practice, perhaps through journaling, in which incidents that precipitate strong emotional reactions are documented and examined. Over time, patterns emerge, revealing the contours of our triggers, the thematic threads that connect disparate events to a cohesive, underlying narrative of vulnerability.

Equipped with this knowledge, the endeavor then shifts to managing these responses, a task that requires both strategy and patience. Initial steps might involve the creation of a psychological buffer, a moment of pause between the trigger and response, allowing for a choice in how to proceed rather than being swept away by the tidal wave of emotion. Techniques such as deep breathing or visualizing a calming scene can serve as anchors, grounding us in the present and mitigating the intensity of the triggered response. Furthermore, cognitive restructuring offers a path to reframe the narrative around the trigger, challenging the validity of the threat it represents and gradually diminishing its power to destabilize.

Yet the true transformation lies not merely in managing these triggers but in the profound growth that arises from this endeavor. Each confrontation with a trigger, each successful navigation through the turbulent waters it conjures, serves as a milestone in the journey towards emotional intelligence. It fosters resilience, an inner strength that emerges from the understanding and mastery of one's emotional responses. Moreover, this journey illuminates the interconnectedness of our emotional triggers with our relationships and interactions, highlighting how the shadows cast by these triggers can shape the dynamics of our engagements with others.

This nuanced understanding of emotional triggers and their management does not culminate in the eradication of these responses. Instead, it heralds a shift in perspective, a recognition of these triggers as signposts guiding us towards deeper self-awareness and emotional maturity. Through this lens, triggers become not just obstacles to be overcome but growth opportunities; each encounter is an invitation to delve deeper into the self, to heal, and to harmonize the discordant notes within our emotional symphony.

As we navigate this complex terrain, let us approach our triggers not with trepidation but with curiosity, a willingness to explore the shadowed corners of our psyche with compassion and openness. This exploration, though challenging, promises rewards of insight and equilibrium, a harmonious balance between emotion and reason that stands as the hallmark of accurate emotional intelligence. In this light, the management of emotional triggers emerges not as a task of suppression but as an act of integration, a weaving of our vulnerabilities into the fabric of our being that enriches our interactions with the world and with ourselves.

From Awareness to Acceptance: Embracing Your Emotional Self

In the nuanced terrain of personal growth, the progression from awareness of one's emotional states to full acceptance of them is not without its hurdles. This transition, while subtle, marks a significant shift in how individuals engage with their inner selves. Recognizing the vast range of one's emotional experiences is one thing; embracing these emotions, with all their complexities and contradictions, demands a different level of engagement. It requires not just observation but also an embrace of one's emotional reality, a willingness to hold space for every facet of one's emotional experience without judgment.

The transition is fraught with challenges. Often, individuals find themselves at odds with their emotions, particularly those that society deems undesirable or inappropriate. Feelings of anger, jealousy, or vulnerability, for example, may be met with internal resistance, a reluctance to acknowledge these emotions as integral components of one's emotional landscape. This resistance stems, in part, from deeply ingrained beliefs about what it means to be emotionally 'healthy' or 'mature.' The notion that some emotions are inherently 'negative' creates a dichotomy that leaves little room for accepting the full emotional spectrum.

Overcoming these challenges requires a reframing of how emotions are perceived. Rather than viewing them through the lens of good versus bad, it becomes necessary to see them as signals, messages from the self that convey needs, desires, and boundaries. This shift in perspective is pivotal; it transforms the relationship with one's emotions from judgment to curiosity. By asking, "What is this emotion telling me?" individuals open a dialogue with their emotional selves, fostering an environment where every emotion is acknowledged and examined.

Central to this process is cultivating self-compassion. This quality, characterized by kindness towards oneself and an understanding of one's experiences as part of the shared human condition, acts as a balm, soothing the often harsh internal critique many harbor against their emotional responses. Self-compassion is not about absolving oneself of responsibility but about recognizing that imperfection and emotional turmoil are inherent aspects of being human. It offers a path to acceptance, one that acknowledges the messiness of emotions while holding space for growth and understanding.

The transformative potential of this journey from awareness to acceptance is illustrated by the experiences of those who have navigated it. Consider, for instance, the story of a young professional who grappled with intense feelings of inadequacy and self-doubt. Despite a successful career, these emotions frequently undermined his sense of accomplishment. Through the practice of emotional journaling, he began to recognize the triggers for these feelings, tracing them back to early experiences of criticism. This awareness, coupled with a deliberate practice of self-compassion, gradually shifted his perspective. He learned to greet his feelings of inadequacy with kindness, viewing them as opportunities for self-compassion rather than evidence of failure. This shift did not erase his feelings of self-doubt overnight, but it allowed him to engage with them in a way that was healing rather than harmful.

Another example is found in a retired educator who, in her solitude, confronted feelings of loneliness and grief following the loss of her partner. For months, she resisted these emotions, viewing them as weaknesses. It was only when she allowed herself to fully experience her grief, acknowledging it as a testament to her love rather than a flaw in her character, that she found a measure of peace. This acceptance was facilitated by her participation in a support group, where the shared experiences of loss and healing fostered a sense of common humanity, underscoring the role of compassion in the journey towards emotional acceptance.

These stories highlight the nuanced process of embracing one's emotional self, marked by challenges but also profound opportunities for growth. They underscore the importance of reframing how emotions are perceived, recognizing them as integral to the human experience. Moreover, they illustrate the pivotal role of self-compassion in facilitating acceptance, offering a gentle reminder that kindness towards oneself is not indulgence but a necessary component of emotional health.

As this chapter concludes, the journey from awareness to acceptance of one's emotional self emerges as a critical aspect of personal development. It is a path that requires patience, curiosity, and, above all, compassion. By approaching our emotions with this level of engagement, we not only elevate our emotional intelligence but also forge a deeper bond with our inner selves and the intricate mosaic of human emotions. This process, while deeply personal, echoes the universal quest for understanding and acceptance, a quest that continues to unfold in the chapters that follow.

Real-World Examples and Case Studies for Self-Reflection Techniques

Example of Meditation in Action: A Busy Professional's Routine

Take, for instance, Sarah, a project manager who begins each morning with a ten-minute meditation session. In the high-paced world of project management, Sarah found herself constantly stressed and reactive, especially in morning meetings. By incorporating a brief meditation practice, she learned to clear her mind and focus on her breath, centering herself before her day even began. Over time, she noticed that this simple practice helped her identify the stress triggers that typically surfaced during meetings, such as tight deadlines or unexpected changes.

Through this awareness, Sarah developed a habit of taking three deep breaths before responding to challenging situations. This new approach helped her maintain composure and positively influence the atmosphere of her meetings, turning moments of potential frustration into opportunities for calm, clear-headed communication. Sarah's practice highlights how meditation can serve as a foundational tool for emotional self-regulation, empowering professionals to approach their work with greater intentionality and less stress.

Journaling for Emotional Insight: A Teacher's Journey

Consider Mark, a high school teacher who struggled with frustration over disruptive classroom behavior. On a colleague's advice, Mark started keeping a daily journal in which he recorded his emotions after each class. Through journaling, he began to recognize patterns in his responses, identifying specific student behaviors that triggered feelings of impatience and stress.

As he reflected on these patterns, Mark realized he could preemptively address some triggers by modifying his teaching approach. He began to implement brief, calming breathing exercises at the start of each class, which helped both him and his students settle into a focused mindset. Mark's commitment to journaling not only provided him with a greater sense of control but also created a more positive, supportive classroom environment. This case study underscores the power of journaling as a self-reflective tool, enabling individuals to identify emotional triggers and cultivate effective strategies to manage them.

Feedback Loops and Journaling in Professional Growth

In another example, we look at John, a marketing executive who recognized the need to improve his interpersonal skills. He asked his colleagues for feedback on his communication style, receiving honest insights on areas where he came across as dismissive or impatient. John used journaling to process this feedback, writing down instances where he noticed these tendencies and reflecting on his emotional state at the time.

By consistently tracking his reactions, John began to notice a pattern: he was often dismissive when he felt his ideas weren't being heard. Armed with this insight, he worked to pause and listen actively during conversations, validating others' input before sharing his own thoughts. Over several months, John's journaling practice helped him reshape his approach, resulting in more harmonious working relationships and a stronger, more collaborative team environment.

His story illustrates how journaling can be used to incorporate feedback effectively, making it a valuable tool for professional growth.

Long-Term Transformation through Self-Reflection

Finally, let's consider Emily, a senior manager in the healthcare field, who committed to journaling and meditation for a whole year to manage workplace stress. By setting aside ten minutes each morning to meditate and fifteen minutes each evening to journal, Emily developed an awareness of her stress triggers and how she responded emotionally throughout the day.

Over time, Emily noticed her responses changing. She became more resilient and able to address high-stress situations without the anxiety that had previously overwhelmed her. Her journal entries reflected a gradual transformation: she moved from frustration and self-doubt to a more centered, confident leadership style. This example demonstrates how combining meditation and journaling as self-reflective practices can lead to lasting emotional growth and improved workplace effectiveness.

Practical Exercise for Readers

To apply these techniques in your own life, consider starting with this exercise:

- Tonight, set aside ten minutes to journal about a recent situation where you felt emotionally reactive. Describe the problem, your emotional response, and what triggered it. Reflect on how you might approach a similar scenario with greater self-awareness and composure.
- Or try a five-minute mindfulness meditation before bed. As you meditate, pay attention to any recurring thoughts or emotions, acknowledging them without judgment. Then, journal about your experience, noting any insights or patterns that arose. This practice can help you build a foundation for

self-reflection, empowering you to manage your emotions more effectively in the future.

Chapter Summary: Self-Reflection – The Unseen Mirror

Introduction to Self-Reflection

- Self-reflection is the foundational step in developing emotional intelligence, akin to navigating an ocean with tools like a compass and a map. It allows us to explore our emotions and motivations with curiosity rather than judgment, giving us the clarity needed to manage our responses and understand how our emotions impact those around us.

The Importance of Self-Reflection

- At the core of EI, self-reflection involves turning our attention inward to examine the motives and emotions that drive our behaviors. This process, much like a lighthouse guiding sailors, helps illuminate patterns in our thoughts and feelings, empowering us with greater control and self-awareness in our journey towards emotional intelligence.

Techniques for Self-Reflection: Meditation and Journaling

- Meditation and journaling are two practical tools for introspection:
    - **Meditation** invites silence and focus, enabling a calm, detached observation of thoughts and emotions as they arise. Starting with five minutes daily and focusing on the breath can help cultivate this mindful awareness.
    - **Journaling** provides a structured way to document emotions and thoughts. Writing about daily emotional

experiences offers insight into personal triggers and patterns, reinforcing self-awareness.

Feedback Loops: Enhancing Self-Awareness Through Feedback

- Feedback from others acts as a mirror, reflecting how others perceive our emotional responses. Seeking feedback with specific questions helps validate or challenge our self-perceptions. This loop of asking, receiving, and incorporating feedback, especially from trusted sources, plays a vital role in building a more comprehensive view of our emotional presence.

Real-Life Case Studies of Self-Reflection

- Self-reflection can lead to transformative change, as illustrated by examples:
  - A professor who, through journaling and meditation, revitalized her teaching style based on feedback.
  - Individuals who use self-reflection to manage triggers respond to challenges more effectively.
  - These cases demonstrate that integrating feedback and introspective practices can enhance self-awareness and EI, paving the way for personal and professional growth.

Emotional Journaling: Mapping the Emotional Landscape

- **Emotional Journaling** involves regularly documenting emotions to understand patterns and triggers. This practice goes beyond recording events to focus on processing emotions, which helps reduce stress and anxiety. Consistent journaling allows for the recognition of emotional patterns, fostering empathy, and encouraging self-compassion.
- **Benefits**: Enhanced self-awareness, stress reduction, and improved emotional regulation.

- **Getting Started**: Use prompts like "Today, I felt ___ because ___" to guide entries and engage with this practice daily. Over time, the journal serves as a repository of insights, supporting personal growth and emotional resilience.

The Role of Pattern Recognition in Emotional Growth

- Over time, reviewing journal entries reveals recurring emotional responses, enabling the identification of triggers and habitual reactions. Recognizing these patterns is the first step in managing emotional responses, allowing us to anticipate and adjust our behavior in future scenarios.

The Power of Mindfulness in Cultivating Self-Awareness

- Mindfulness, the practice of observing the present moment without judgment, is crucial for deepening self-awareness. By focusing on the here and now, mindfulness helps us connect with our thoughts, emotions, and bodily sensations, enhancing clarity and understanding.
- **Mindfulness Practices**: Techniques such as mindful breathing, body scans, and object-focused observation anchor attention in the present. These practices refine our awareness and enable us to observe emotional responses without becoming overwhelmed by them.
- **Impact on EI**: Regular mindfulness practice enhances self-awareness and self-regulation, promotes empathy, and sharpens social skills, making it a valuable tool in developing EI.

Identifying Emotional Triggers

- Emotional triggers are stimuli that evoke strong emotions. These triggers often stem from past experiences or unresolved conflicts and influence our reactions in the present.

- The process of identifying triggers involves observing emotional shifts, documenting responses, and recognizing patterns. Effective management techniques include pausing before reacting, practicing deep breathing, and reframing thoughts to reduce the impact of triggers.

From Awareness to Acceptance: Embracing Your Emotional Self

- Transitioning from awareness to acceptance is essential in personal growth. This process involves embracing all emotions, even those perceived as negative, as integral to the human experience.
- **Challenges and Self-Compassion**: Society often labels emotions such as anger and vulnerability as negative, leading to self-judgment. Reframing emotions as signals rather than weaknesses and approaching them with self-compassion facilitates acceptance.
- **Examples**: Stories of individuals who use self-compassion to overcome feelings of inadequacy or grief highlight the importance of this acceptance. By accepting emotions without judgment, they experience healing and growth, illustrating how self-compassion and acceptance contribute to a deeper connection with one's emotional self.

Conclusion

Self-reflection and mindfulness are key practices in developing emotional intelligence. Together, they foster self-awareness, acceptance, and growth. Embracing one's emotions without judgment, approaching them with curiosity, and recognizing their role as guides in personal development lead to greater emotional maturity and fulfillment.

THREE

THE ALCHEMY OF SELF-REGULATION

In the stillness of a serene morning, as the world stirs awake and the mind oscillates between the remnants of dreams and the day's impending realities, lies the perfect tableau for understanding emotional regulation. It's in these quiet moments that the subtleties of our emotional landscape come into focus, revealing the interplay between our inner world and the external stimuli that beckon responses, both measured and impetuous. This chapter delves into the nuanced art of emotional regulation, an endeavor as critical as it is challenging, offering insights and strategies to navigate the tumultuous waters of our emotions with finesse and empowering you with a sense of control over your emotional responses.

The Art of Emotional Regulation: Techniques That Work

Importance of Emotional Regulation

The capacity to modulate emotions, to steer them with intent rather than be steered by them, underpins not only our mental and emotional well-being but also influences the quality of our interactions and relationships. Effective emotional regulation involves recognizing our emotional triggers, understanding the responses they invoke, and consciously choosing how we express these emotions. Like a skilled gardener who knows just when to water and when to prune, adept emotional regulation ensures our emotional landscape is both vibrant and sustainable.

Techniques for Regulation

Cognitive Reappraisal

Cognitive reappraisal is akin to changing the lens through which we view a situation, altering its emotional impact. Imagine standing before a vast, tumultuous ocean, the waves a metaphor for our distressing emotions. Cognitive reappraisal invites us to see not just the chaos of crashing waves but also the vastness of the ocean itself, reminding us of the broader context and the transient nature of our emotional states. This technique hinges on the idea that our interpretations shape our emotions; changing those interpretations changes the emotional response, offering a beacon of hope in the face of emotional turmoil.

Practically, when faced with a challenging situation, ask, "Is there another way to view this?" Consider a work scenario where criticism feels personal and harsh. Cognitive reappraisal encourages a shift in perspective, viewing the critique not as an attack but as valuable feedback aimed at growth and improvement.

Cognitive reappraisal involves reframing the way we perceive a situation to change its emotional impact. This method is highly effective for managing negative emotions and fostering a more positive or neutral response. Here's how you can practice cognitive reappraisal in a few simple steps:

- **Step 1: Identify the Triggering Thought**
  - Recognize when you feel a strong emotional reaction. Note the specific thought or belief that triggered this

feeling. For example, if you're upset because a coworker dismissed your idea in a meeting, identify the thought, "They don't respect my input."

- **Step 2: Question the Thought**
  - Challenge the accuracy of this thought. Ask yourself, "Is there evidence to support this belief?" or "Are there alternative explanations for what happened?" Perhaps your coworker was preoccupied or unaware of how their response came across.
- **Step 3: Reframe the Thought**
  - Now, consciously reframe the situation to consider a more balanced perspective. You might think, "It's possible they were focused on something else and didn't realize how they sounded," or "My ideas are valuable, and I'll seek other ways to share them with the team." This new perspective can significantly lessen negative feelings and lead to a more constructive approach.
- **Step 4: Reinforce the Reframe**
  - Each time you think back on the situation, remind yourself of your new, more balanced perspective. With practice, reframing can become second nature, helping you manage reactions to triggering events more healthily.

Emotional Distancing

Emotional distancing is a technique that involves creating a psychological space between ourselves and our emotional reactions. It's like taking a step back from our feelings and looking at them from a distance. This allows us to view our feelings with a degree of detachment, which can reduce their immediacy and intensity.

In moments of heightened emotion, try visualizing yourself as a spectator to your emotional experience, observing without judgment or engagement. This perspective can cool the heat of the moment, providing room to choose a more considered response.

Emotional distancing allows you to step back from a situation and assess it objectively rather than reacting impulsively. This technique is instrumental in high-stress situations where emotions may cloud judgment. Here's a step-by-step guide to emotional distancing:

- **Step 1: Take a Pause**
  - When you feel an intense emotion, consciously pause. This might mean taking a deep breath or stepping away from the situation temporarily, such as going for a short walk or simply counting to ten.
- **Step 2: Observe Without Judgment**
  - Try to view the situation as an outsider. Ask yourself, "How would I perceive this if I were an observer rather than someone involved?" For instance, if you're upset over a disagreement with a friend, imagine how a neutral third party might view the conversation.
- **Step 3: Name the Emotion**
  - Labeling your emotion can help create a sense of distance. Say to yourself, "I'm feeling frustrated right now," or "I'm experiencing disappointment." Recognizing the specific emotion helps reduce its intensity by moving your brain into a more analytical mode.
- **Step 4: Reflect on the Bigger Picture**
  - Shift your focus to the broader context. Ask yourself, "Will this matter a year from now?" or "What are my long-term goals with this person or situation?" This step helps you maintain perspective, reminding you that a single moment doesn't define an entire relationship or outcome.
- **Step 5: Choose a Constructive Response**
  - Now that you've created some mental space, decide how you want to respond. Think about actions that align with your values and desired outcomes. For example, instead of reacting defensively, you might calmly express how you feel or choose to revisit the topic when emotions have cooled down.

- **Step 6: Practice Self-Compassion**
  - After you've responded, reflect on your reaction and the outcome without harsh self-criticism. Self-regulation is a skill that improves with practice, and acknowledging your efforts, even if they don't feel perfect, is crucial to strengthening this technique over time.

Practical Applications

Incorporating these techniques into daily life enhances our emotional agility, fostering a resilience that buffers against the vicissitudes of life. When a situation sparks an immediate emotional reaction, pause. Breathe. Employ cognitive reappraisal to assess alternative interpretations or adopt emotional distancing to gain perspective. Over time, these practices become reflexive, a part of our emotional repertoire that enriches our interactions and deepens our understanding of ourselves.

Building a Regulation Toolkit

Creating a personalized emotional regulation toolkit is akin to assembling a set of keys, each unlocking different aspects of emotional mastery. Start by identifying emotions that frequently challenge your equilibrium. For each, devise a strategy based on cognitive reappraisal or emotional distancing tailored to your experiences and triggers, ensuring that you feel understood and catered to in your journey towards emotional balance.

Consider maintaining a journal to document instances of emotional upheaval and the techniques you apply. Reflect on the outcomes and refine your approach as you discover what resonates with your unique emotional landscape. This journal becomes not only a record of growth but a resource for future encounters, a testament to your evolving capability for emotional regulation.

Daily Practice: Building Self-Regulation into Your Routine

Incorporate these techniques into your daily routine with simple practices:

- **Morning Mindset Check:** Set intentions for your day in a few minutes each morning. Ask yourself, "What emotions do I want to embody today?" and visualize yourself responding calmly to potential stressors.
- **Reflection Journal:** At the end of each day, write about a situation where you practiced cognitive reappraisal or emotional distancing. Document how you felt initially, what steps you took, and the outcome. Over time, you'll notice patterns and progress in your ability to manage emotions.
- **Set Reminders:** Use reminders on your phone or notes on your workspace that say, "Pause and reframe" or "Step back and observe." These cues can help reinforce self-regulation practices throughout the day.

Visualization Exercise: The Emotional Compass

Imagine standing within a sprawling forest, where the canopy above weaves sunlight into a complex pattern of shadows and light. Your emotions are the forest, vast and intricate. Within your hand lies a compass, its needle poised to guide you through this terrain. This compass represents your capacity for emotional regulation, a tool that, when used with intent, can navigate the most bewildering of emotional landscapes. As you move through the forest, let the compass guide you, steering clear of thorny underbrush and tangled vines, and seeking paths that offer clarity and perspective. This visualization encapsulates the essence of emotional regulation; navigating our emotions with purpose, guided by the tools of cognitive reappraisal and emotional distancing, ensuring that even in the heart of the forest, we find our way.

This chapter unfolds the complexities of emotional regulation, presenting it not as a destination but as a process, a continuous engagement with our emotional selves. Through the techniques and practices shared, the art of emotional regulation emerges as a critical, though attainable, aspect of emotional intelligence, a skill that enriches our lives and deepens our connections with ourselves and others.

Visualization Exercise: The "Calm Waters"

The **Calm Waters** technique uses visualization to guide you through self-regulation. It helps you internalize the practice of managing emotions by visualizing yourself in a calm, stable place where you can observe and address your feelings with clarity.

1. **Find a Quiet Space**
   - Sit comfortably in a place where you won't be disturbed. Close your eyes, take a deep breath, and let your shoulders relax. Begin by taking three slow, deep breaths, focusing on the sensation of the air entering and leaving your body. Allow your mind to settle and your focus to shift inward.
2. **Visualize a Peaceful Body of Water**
   - Picture yourself standing beside a calm, serene lake. The water is still, reflecting the sky above with perfect clarity. This lake represents your inner self, your natural state of calm and balance. Notice how the water feels tranquil, undisturbed, and peaceful.
3. **Imagine Throwing a Stone into the Water**
   - Now, imagine holding a small stone in your hand. This stone represents a challenging emotion you're currently experiencing; perhaps it's frustration, sadness, or anxiety. Visualize yourself gently tossing the stone into the water. As it hits the surface, notice the ripples that form and expand across the lake.
4. **Observe the Ripples and Your Response**
   - Watch as the ripples move outward, gradually slowing until the lake returns to its original calm state. Imagine that the ripples represent your initial emotional reaction. Recognize that it's natural to feel these ripples, but that

they are temporary. As the ripples fade, remind yourself that you can return to a place of calm and balance.

5. **Use Your Breath to Settle the Water**
   - As the ripples diminish, focus on your breathing. With each inhale, imagine that you're drawing in a sense of peace and stability. With each exhale, imagine that you're releasing tension and emotional turbulence. Picture the water becoming even smoother with every breath until it's completely calm once more.

6. **Affirm Your Inner Calm**
   - When the water is still, silently repeat a calming affirmation to yourself, such as:
     - "I am in control of my emotions."
     - "I can observe my feelings without letting them overwhelm me."
     - "My inner calm is always within reach."

7. **Reflect and Return**
   - Take a moment to reflect on how you feel, knowing that, just as the lake returns to calm after an emotional ripple, you can too. When you're ready, slowly open your eyes and bring your awareness back to the present moment.

Practice Tip: Use this visualization exercise whenever you need to regulate your emotions. By repeatedly practicing the **Calm Waters** technique, you'll strengthen your ability to approach challenging situations with a sense of control and resilience. Over time, this exercise will become a mental anchor, helping you manage emotions effectively and consistently.

Stress Management for the Modern World

In an era where the digital and the tangible intertwine, stress has morphed into a ubiquitous shadow, tailing us through the relentless pace of modern life. From the incessant pings of our devices beckoning our attention to the high-wire act of balancing personal and professional responsibilities, the sources of stress are as varied as they are pervasive. This landscape, marked by its relentless demand for our time, attention, and energy, necessitates a reevaluation of our strategies for managing stress, embedding these practices not as occasional retreats from the world but as integral components of our daily lives.

Modern Stressors

The canvas of today's stressors is vast, painted with the broad strokes of technological advancements and the finer details of individual life circumstances. At one end lies the pressure cooker of the workplace, where deadlines, expectations, and competition create a simmering broth of anxiety. At the other, personal relationships and self-imposed standards of success and happiness add layers of complexity to the emotional mix. The intersection of these dimensions, compounded by the constant connectivity afforded by smartphones and social media, leaves little room for respite, creating a milieu where stress not only thrives but proliferates.

Stress Management Techniques

Navigating this landscape demands a toolkit that is both versatile and personal, capable of addressing the multifaceted nature of modern stress. Mindfulness meditation emerges as a beacon in this regard, offering a port in the storm through its invitation to anchor ourselves in the present moment. This practice, rooted in the breath, serves as a counterbalance to the centrifugal forces of stress, drawing us back from the precipice of our worries about the future and regrets over the past.

Equally potent is the practice of physical activity, a catharsis for the pent-up energy that stress so often engenders. Whether it's a brisk walk in the embrace of nature or a sweat-drenched gym session, movement offers a release valve for stress, channeling it into physical exertion and dissipating its hold on our mental and emotional well-being.

Mastering time management is also essential in the array of stress management approaches. By effectively allocating time, setting achievable objectives, and balancing work and relaxation, we create a structured environment that helps mitigate stress. This approach not only keeps stress at manageable levels but also supports a harmonious life by recognizing and managing it without letting it take over. By prioritizing tasks, setting realistic goals, and carving out dedicated periods for work and rest, we construct a framework within which stress can be contained and managed rather than allowed to run rampant. This structure, far from constricting, provides the scaffolding for a balanced life, one where stress is acknowledged but not permitted to dominate.

Creating a Stress Management Plan

The construction of a personalized stress management plan begins with a foundation of self-awareness and an inventory of the stressors that most frequently disturb our equilibrium. This detailed, honest mapping allows identification of patterns and triggers, laying the groundwork for targeted interventions.

From this foundation, we select from the array of available techniques those that resonate most with our lifestyle, preferences, and the specific nature of our stressors. This selection process is iterative, a continuous refinement based on effectiveness and personal affinity. Each technique, once chosen, is woven into the fabric of our daily routines, becoming an integral part of our lives.

The linchpin of this plan is adaptability, an openness to revision and change as circumstances evolve and new stressors emerge. This flexibility ensures that our stress management plan remains a living document responsive to the shifting landscapes of our lives.

The Role of EI in Stress Management

The threads connecting emotional intelligence to effective stress management are both numerous and profound. At its core, emotional intelligence equips us to recognize and understand our emotional responses to stress, offering a map for navigating our internal landscapes. This awareness, when coupled with the skills of emotional regulation, allows us to modulate our responses to stressors, tempering their impact and reducing their emotional toll.

Moreover, emotional intelligence fosters empathy for ourselves and others, engendering a compassionate approach to stress. This empathy illuminates the shared nature of our struggles, offering solace in the knowledge that we are not alone in our experiences of stress and anxiety.

In the crucible of stress management, emotional intelligence acts as both a shield and a sword, protecting us from the onslaught of stressors while equipping us with the strategies to counter them. It is through this lens that the practices of mindfulness, physical activity, and time management gain their fullest expression, not merely as techniques for alleviating stress but as expressions of a deeper engagement with our emotional selves.

In this intricate dance with stress, our emotional intelligence guides our steps, ensuring that even when the music accelerates, we move with grace and intention, turning the challenge of stress management into an opportunity for growth and resilience.

Anger Management: Constructive Coping Strategies

In the intricate dance of human emotions, anger often takes center stage with its vibrant intensity and undeniable presence. This potent force, while universally experienced, spans from a whisper of irritation to the roar of rage, influencing interactions and shaping the contours of both personal and professional landscapes. The exploration of anger, its roots, manifestations, and the paths to its regulation presents an opportunity for profound self-discovery and transformation.

Understanding Anger

At its core, anger is a primal response, a protective mechanism that signals a perceived threat or injustice. Its power lies not in its existence but in its expression, the manner in which it is communicated and acted upon. The impact of unbridled anger on relationships is profound, eroding trust, fostering resentment, and often leading to the disintegration of meaningful connections. In professional settings, the repercussions of anger mismanagement can cascade, affecting teamwork, leadership perception, and overall workplace harmony. Recognizing anger as both a natural and necessary emotion is the first step in reframing its role from a disruptive force to a catalyst for positive change.

Anger Triggers

Identifying personal triggers for anger is akin to mapping the minefields of one's emotional terrain. These triggers are deeply personal, rooted in past experiences, values, and vulnerabilities. For some, criticism, whether constructive or not, ignites anger, perceived as a direct assault on their competence or worth. For others, feelings of disrespect or injustice, whether real or perceived, act as a spark. The process of uncovering these triggers demands honesty and introspection, a willingness to probe the depths of one's experiences and reactions. This exploration, while challenging, illuminates the patterns of anger, offering insights into its origins and providing the foundation for effective management strategies.

Coping Mechanisms

The cultivation of constructive coping mechanisms for anger management is a dynamic process, one that requires experimentation and adaptation. One effective strategy is the practice of 'time-outs,' a deliberate pause in the heat of anger's grip, which allows emotions to cool and responses to be recalibrated. This pause creates a space for reflection, a moment to question the validity of the anger and the appropriateness of potential reactions.

Another technique involves deliberately altering the physical responses that accompany anger. Deep, controlled breathing, a simple yet powerful tool, counters the rapid heart rate and heightened adrenaline characteristic of anger, promoting a state of calm and reducing the intensity of the emotion. Similarly, engaging in physical activities, such as a brisk walk or a vigorous workout, serves as an outlet for the excess energy anger generates, facilitating a return to equilibrium.

The strategy of expressive writing offers another avenue for coping with anger. Through the written word, emotions can be articulated, explored, and ultimately understood. This practice, far from a mere venting of frustrations, encourages a structured examination of the anger, its triggers, and the underlying reasons for its intensity. By transferring these thoughts and feelings onto paper, the individual gains a measure of control, transforming anger from an overwhelming force into a manageable emotion.

From Anger to Advocacy

Perhaps the most transformative approach to anger management is the channeling of this emotion into positive action and advocacy. Anger, in its essence, signals a passion, a deep care for an issue or injustice. When harnessed constructively, this passion becomes a driving force for change, motivating actions and initiatives to address the root causes of the anger. This process begins with identifying the issue at the heart of the anger, followed by strategic planning of steps to effect change. Whether through advocacy, volunteering, or initiating dialogue and awareness around the issue, the energy of anger can fuel efforts that contribute to meaningful, positive outcomes.

The transition from anger to advocacy requires a shift in perspective: viewing anger not as an enemy to be suppressed but as a resource to be leveraged. It demands a balance between emotion and reason, ensuring that actions taken are not only driven by passion but guided by thoughtful consideration and strategic planning. This balance ensures that the advocacy efforts are constructive, targeted, and effective, turning the potential destructiveness of anger into a force for good.

In navigating the complexities of anger, the recognition of its dual nature as both a challenge and an opportunity is crucial. By embracing anger as a natural part of the emotional spectrum, identifying personal triggers, adopting constructive coping strategies, and channeling its energy into advocacy and positive action, individuals can transform their relationship with this potent emotion. This transformation from anger to advocacy represents not merely a coping mechanism but a profound shift in how anger is perceived and utilized, marking a step towards emotional maturity and a deeper engagement with the issues that ignite passion and drive change.

Overcoming Anxiety: Tools for Calm

In today's rapidly changing world, where life's pace quickens by the day and information overload is a constant, anxiety has become a common shadow for many, subtly instilling doubts and fears. This phenomenon, pervasive across the globe, reflects not merely personal susceptibilities but the very nature of contemporary society; a world where the expectation to perform, achieve, and be perpetually connected creates fertile ground for anxiety to flourish. The acknowledgment of this reality, however, is not an acquiescence to its dominion but the first step in reclaiming calm from the clutches of anxious thoughts and feelings.

In the quest to mitigate the grip of anxiety, a constellation of tools and techniques stands ready, each offering a pathway to tranquility. Among these, breathing exercises and visualization emerge as beacons of relief, guiding individuals through the turbulence of anxious states to the serenity of a centered mind. Breathing exercises, in their simplicity, wield a profound power. The deliberate slowing and deepening of breath acts as a direct line to the body's relaxation response, a counterforce to the surge of adrenaline that anxiety so often provokes. This practice, when practiced regularly, serves as an anchor in moments of anxiety, a tangible action that beckons the mind away from the precipice of panic.

Visualization, or the mental construction of peaceful, calming images and scenarios, operates in the mind's eye, offering an escape from the immediate triggers of anxiety. By envisioning oneself in a serene setting, a lush forest bathed in the golden light of dawn or a quiet beach where the rhythm of the waves matches the breath, individuals can transport their consciousness to a place of tranquility, if only momentarily. This technique not only diverts attention from the source of anxiety but also fosters a mental environment where calm can be cultivated.

However, the effectiveness of these tools is magnified when they are personalized and tailored to align with the individual's unique experiences, triggers, and preferences. Personalization begins with an attentive exploration of one's encounters with anxiety, identifying not just the triggers but the physical sensations, thoughts, and emotions that accompany anxious states. Armed with this insight, individuals can adapt breathing exercises to their rhythm, choosing techniques that resonate with their physiological responses and craft visualizations that draw on their memories and aspirations, creating mental sanctuaries that hold particular power over their anxieties.

The role of emotional intelligence (EI) in this process is both profound and multifaceted, acting as a catalyst for more effective anxiety management. At its heart, EI offers a deeper understanding of the emotional landscape within which anxiety resides, illuminating the patterns of thought and feeling that feed into anxious states. This awareness, when combined with the emotional regulation skills EI fosters, enables individuals to approach their anxiety with a sense of agency, choosing responses that acknowledge the emotion while gently steering the self towards equilibrium.

Moreover, EI enhances the capacity for empathy, both towards oneself and others, infusing the journey through anxiety with a compassion that eases the journey. This empathetic stance encourages a kinder, more forgiving approach to personal struggles with anxiety, countering the self-criticism that so often exacerbates anxious feelings. It also fosters a sense of connection, a recognition that one's experiences of anxiety are shared by many, reducing feelings of isolation and offering solace in the knowledge that others, too, navigate this challenging terrain.

In the cultivation of EI, mindfulness emerges as a key practice, a tool that not only bolsters self-awareness but also strengthens the ability to regulate emotional responses. Mindfulness, with its emphasis on present-moment awareness, encourages a non-judgmental acceptance of anxious thoughts and feelings, observing them as they arise and pass without becoming ensnared. This practice, integrated into daily life, transforms the relationship with anxiety from one of struggle and resistance to one of acceptance and management.

The synergy between EI and anxiety management techniques, such as breathing exercises, visualization, and mindfulness, creates a holistic approach to overcoming anxiety. This approach does not seek to eliminate anxiety, an unrealistic and perhaps even undesirable goal, given anxiety's role as a signal of underlying needs or concerns. Instead, it aims to reduce the distress anxiety causes, to manage its intensity and frequency, and to cultivate a sense of calm and resilience in its wake.

In navigating the complexities of anxiety in the modern context, the tools and techniques shared here offer not just a reprieve but a roadmap to a more serene state of being. Through personalized application and the cultivation of emotional intelligence, individuals can navigate the maze of anxiety, emerging with a renewed sense of peace and a strengthened capacity to face life's challenges with equanimity.

Building Resilience:
Bouncing Back Stronger

Resilience, a term often evoked in the narratives of survival and triumph, encapsulates the profound ability to recover from setbacks, adapt to change, and keep going in the face of adversity. Within the framework of emotional intelligence, resilience is the bedrock upon which the edifice of personal growth and professional success is built. It is the force that propels individuals forward, not despite the challenges they face but because of them. This quality, both inherent and cultivated, enables individuals to navigate the complexities of life with a steadfastness that is both admirable and crucial to well-being.

In the quest to fortify this inherent resilience, several strategies emerge as pivotal. One such approach involves a shift in mindset, a reorientation of perspective that views challenges not as insurmountable obstacles but as opportunities for growth. This perspective, rooted in the principles of positive psychology, champions the role of adversity in shaping character and competence. It encourages individuals to approach setbacks with a sense of curiosity and openness, asking not "Why is this happening to me?" but "What can I learn from this?" This reframing of experiences, from negative to potentially positive, lays the groundwork for a resilient response, transforming the narrative from one of victimhood to one of agency and empowerment.

Another cornerstone of resilience architecture is cultivating a robust support network. Human beings, inherently social creatures, thrive on connection and community. The strength derived from relationships, be they familial, platonic, or professional, cannot be overstated. These bonds, characterized by mutual respect, empathy, and understanding, provide a safety net that cushions the fall during times of trouble. They offer solace, advice, and a sounding board for the fears and frustrations that inevitably arise in the face of adversity. Moreover, the act of reaching out for support, far from a sign of weakness, is a testament to the strength and wisdom in recognizing the value of collective resilience over individual fortitude.

Resilience in action is best exemplified by real-life narratives that underscore its transformative power. Consider the entrepreneur who, after facing the collapse of a once-thriving business, uses the lessons learned from failure to build a new venture, this time with a foundation stronger and more flexible than before. Or the artist who, after years of rejection, finds solace and strength in a community of fellow creatives, eventually breaking through to critical acclaim. These stories, diverse in their details, share a common thread: the indomitable spirit of resilience that fuels the journey from setback to success.

Maintaining resilience through life's myriad challenges requires more than just a strong will; it necessitates a toolkit of strategies that can be called upon when needed. Regular self-care practices, including mindfulness, exercise, and adequate rest, serve as maintenance for the mind and body, ensuring that one is physically and mentally prepared to face stressors. Continuous learning and skill development also play a crucial role, as they equip individuals with the tools to navigate changing landscapes. Perhaps most importantly, the practice of gratitude, focusing on the positives even in the midst of adversity, fosters a sense of perspective that is essential to resilience. It is this combination of self-care, continuous growth, and gratitude that sustains resilience, enabling individuals to not just bounce back from adversity but to leap forward, stronger and wiser than before.

As this chapter on resilience concludes, the strategies and narratives presented collectively form a robust framework of strength and adaptability. From the transformative potential of a mindset shift to the foundational support of relationships, the building and maintenance of resilience are revealed as both an art and a science. It is a dynamic process, continuously shaped by experiences and choices, that stands at the heart of emotional intelligence. As we transition from the contemplation of resilience to the broader exploration of emotional intelligence in action, let us carry forward the lessons of resilience: the courage to face adversity, the wisdom to learn from it, and the strength to emerge from it, not just intact but invigorated.

Chapter Summary: The Alchemy of Self-Regulation

Introduction to Self-Regulation

- Self-regulation is the ability to manage one's emotional responses and behaviors, an essential aspect of emotional intelligence. In moments of quiet reflection, we can see the interplay between our inner world and external stimuli, allowing us to respond intentionally rather than impulsively. This chapter explores techniques for mastering self-regulation, providing tools to navigate emotions with clarity and control.

The Art of Emotional Regulation

- Self-regulation is crucial for emotional well-being and positively impacts our interactions and relationships. Much like a gardener tends to plants, regulating emotions requires careful attention, pruning adverse reactions and nurturing positive ones to create a balanced emotional state.

Techniques for Emotional Regulation

- **Cognitive Reappraisal**: This involves changing the way we interpret a situation to alter its emotional impact. For example, viewing criticism as constructive feedback rather than a personal attack helps neutralize negative emotions. By shifting perspective, we can reduce emotional intensity and cultivate resilience.

- **Emotional Distancing**: By mentally stepping back from a situation, we gain perspective on our emotions, allowing us to view them objectively. Visualizing oneself as an observer of the emotion rather than a participant creates a psychological buffer, reducing the immediate intensity and fostering thoughtful responses.

Practical Applications

- Incorporating self-regulation techniques into daily life, such as pausing before reacting or reframing interpretations of events, helps develop emotional resilience. These practices, when applied consistently, become second nature and enhance our ability to engage with life's challenges constructively.

Building a Regulation Toolkit

- A personalized emotional regulation toolkit is essential for navigating a range of emotional challenges. This toolkit can include strategies like cognitive reappraisal, emotional distancing, and journaling. By documenting emotionally charged experiences and reflecting on effective coping strategies, individuals create a resource for future reference and growth.

Visualization Exercise: The Emotional Compass

- Visualization exercises, such as imagining oneself in a forest with an emotional compass, help guide us through the complexities of our emotions. This mental imagery emphasizes the role of self-regulation in navigating emotional landscapes, fostering a sense of inner guidance and direction.

Stress Management for the Modern World

- Modern life introduces numerous stressors, from constant connectivity to personal and professional pressures. The relentless pace and demands of today's world necessitate effective stress management strategies integrated into our daily routines, helping to reduce the cumulative toll of stress.

Techniques for Managing Stress

- **Mindfulness Meditation**: By focusing on the present moment, mindfulness counteracts stress, grounding us and redirecting attention away from worries about the past or future.
- **Physical Activity**: Engaging in regular exercise channels stress into physical exertion, providing a release for pent-up energy and improving overall mental health.
- **Time Management**: Organizing tasks, setting achievable goals, and prioritizing relaxation alongside work helps create a balanced, structured environment. This organization mitigates stress and supports sustained well-being.

Creating a Stress Management Plan

- Developing a personal stress management plan begins with identifying key stressors and recognizing their patterns. By selecting techniques that resonate with one's lifestyle and adapting them over time, individuals build a living document that evolves with changing circumstances.

The Role of EI in Stress Management

- Emotional intelligence (EI) enhances stress management by helping us recognize and understand our emotional responses to stress. This awareness, coupled with empathy and self-regulation skills, allows us to handle stress constructively and develop compassion for ourselves and others.

Anger Management: Constructive Coping Strategies

- Anger, while a natural emotion, can damage relationships and professional standing if unchecked. Understanding its roots and learning constructive coping mechanisms can transform anger from a destructive force into a tool for positive change.

Coping Mechanisms for Anger

- **Time-Outs**: Pausing to reflect during moments of anger provides space to cool down and choose a more thoughtful response.
- **Physical Techniques**: Deep breathing and physical activity help dissipate the physiological arousal that accompanies anger.
- **Expressive Writing**: Writing about anger helps articulate emotions, provides insight, and reduces emotional intensity.

From Anger to Advocacy

- Transforming anger into advocacy involves channeling the passion underlying anger into constructive actions. By addressing the root cause, whether through volunteering or raising awareness, anger becomes a catalyst for meaningful change rather than a source of conflict.

Overcoming Anxiety: Tools for Calm

- Anxiety, a prevalent challenge in modern life, reflects society's demands and expectations. However, it can be managed through techniques like breathing exercises and visualization, which foster calmness and alleviate anxious thoughts.

Anxiety Management Techniques

- **Breathing Exercises**: Deep, slow breaths activate the body's relaxation response, countering anxiety's physiological effects.
- **Visualization**: Mentally creating serene images, such as a peaceful forest, helps divert attention from anxiety triggers, promoting tranquility.
- **Mindfulness**: Practicing present-moment awareness without judgment enables acceptance of anxiety, transforming it from an overwhelming force into a manageable emotion.

Building Resilience: Bouncing Back Stronger

- Resilience is the ability to recover from setbacks and adapt to challenges. This quality is cultivated through mindset shifts, support networks, and a commitment to continuous learning and self-care.

Strategies for Building Resilience

- **Reframe Challenges**: Viewing obstacles as opportunities for growth fosters a resilient mindset, empowering individuals to learn from difficulties.
- **Develop a Support Network**: Connections with others provide emotional support and offer a safety net during tough times.
- **Practice Gratitude**: Focusing on positives, even amid adversity, promotes perspective and strengthens resilience.

Conclusion

The chapter emphasizes that self-regulation is an ongoing process, guiding us through stress, anger, and anxiety. By building emotional regulation skills, individuals deepen their emotional intelligence, transforming personal challenges into opportunities for growth and resilience.

FOUR

DEVELOPING EMPATHY: THE UNSEEN BRIDGE

In an unassuming corner of a bustling city park, where the cacophony of urban life gently fades into a symphony of rustling leaves and distant laughter, a simple yet profound exchange occurs. A young professional, briefcase in hand, pauses to offer a hand to a stranger struggling with an unwieldy stroller. This moment, brief and seemingly inconsequential, encapsulates the essence of empathy: the ability to perceive and resonate with another's emotional state. It is within these spontaneous, often overlooked interactions that the proper depth and potential of empathy are revealed, serving as a testament to its role as a cornerstone of emotional intelligence.

Empathy, with its roots intertwined with notions of understanding and compassion, emerges not as an inherent trait bestowed upon a select few but as a skill ripe for cultivation and refinement. This realization unlocks a realm of possibilities in which empathy extends beyond the confines of personal growth, influencing every interaction and relationship and fostering connections that transcend the superficial to reach the heart of genuine understanding. The role of empathy in personal development is not just significant but empowering, as it allows us to navigate the complexities of human interaction with a heightened sense of self-awareness and understanding. By recognizing the role of empathy in our personal growth, we can empower ourselves to navigate the complexities of human interaction with a heightened sense of self-awareness and understanding.

Walking in Their Shoes: Practical Empathy-Building Exercises

Empathy as a Skill

Empathy, often misconstrued as a mere emotional response, is more accurately understood as a multifaceted skill comprising cognitive and emotional components. Cognitive empathy, the intellectual understanding of another's perspective, complements emotional empathy, the visceral sharing of another's feelings, creating a comprehensive approach to understanding others. This duality underscores the potential for empathy to be honed through deliberate practice, transforming it from a passive capacity to an active pursuit.

Role-Playing Scenarios

Role-playing exercises, a dynamic and engaging method, offer a direct route to enhancing empathy. By stepping into the shoes of another, participants navigate scenarios from perspectives other than their own, confronting challenges, biases, and emotions unfamiliar to their daily lives. Consider, for example, a workplace exercise where employees assume roles outside their departments, tackling tasks and dilemmas from positions they do not ordinarily occupy. This exercise, conducted in a supportive environment, sheds light on the complexities and pressures colleagues face, fostering a culture of mutual understanding and respect.

Empathy Circles

The concept of empathy circles, grounded in the principles of active listening and shared vulnerability, offers another potent avenue for developing empathy. In these gatherings, small groups share personal stories or challenges while others listen intently, refraining from interjections or advice. Following each sharing, listeners reflect on what they heard, not only the content but the emotions and experiences conveyed. This practice, emphasizing understanding over problem-solving, nurtures an environment where empathy flourishes, breaking down barriers and revealing the common humanity that binds us. Empathy circles are a safe space for individuals to share their experiences and feelings and for others to practice active listening and reflection, fostering a deeper understanding and connection among the participants.

Daily Empathy Challenges

Integrating empathy into daily life can be as simple as setting daily empathy challenges. These tasks, designed to be both accessible and impactful, range from engaging in a conversation with someone from a different background to expressing gratitude to those often taken for granted. For instance, you could challenge yourself to have a meaningful conversation with a colleague you don't know well or to actively listen to a friend who is going through a tough time. The act of consciously directing attention towards understanding and connecting with others, even in small ways, cumulatively builds an empathetic lens through which the world is viewed.

Through these exercises, role-playing scenarios, empathy circles, and daily challenges, the skill of empathy is not only developed but celebrated, weaving a thread of understanding and compassion through the fabric of our interactions. The cumulative effect of these practices extends beyond the individual, influencing families, workplaces, and communities, creating ripples that contribute to a more empathetic, connected world.

The development of empathy, as outlined in this chapter, emerges as a transformative process that enriches both the giver and the receiver, bridging divides and fostering connections that underscore our shared humanity. Through deliberate practice and integration into the rhythms of daily life, empathy becomes more than a concept; it becomes a lived experience, a guiding principle that shapes every interaction, every relationship, every moment of connection. In this light, empathy stands not only as a component of emotional intelligence but as a fundamental aspect of what it means to be genuinely human, offering a path to deeper understanding, compassion, and unity in an increasingly complex world. The importance of empathy in resolving conflicts is not just a possibility but a reassurance that even in the most challenging situations, there is hope for understanding and resolution. By understanding the importance of empathy in conflict resolution, we can feel reassured that even in the most challenging situations, there is hope for understanding and resolution.

Reading Emotional Cues: Verbal and Non-Verbal Communication

In the intricate dance of human interaction, the subtleties of emotional expression often speak louder than the words themselves. This nuanced form of communication, woven into the very fabric of our social interactions, relies heavily on the ability to read and interpret both verbal and non-verbal cues. These cues, ranging from the flicker of an expression across a face to the cadence of spoken words, serve as windows into others' emotional states, offering insights that transcend the limitations of language.

The Power of Non-Verbal Cues

The realm of non-verbal communication, vast and largely unspoken, operates on the periphery of our conscious awareness, yet its impact on understanding emotions is profound. Facial expressions, often the most direct indicators of emotion, can convey a spectrum of feelings with subtlety and immediacy. A furrowed brow or a fleeting smile can unveil sentiments unspoken, revealing layers of emotion that words might fail to capture. Similarly, posture and body language offer clues to an individual's emotional state: closed, protective stances indicate discomfort or unease, while open, relaxed postures suggest confidence and openness. Variations in tone of voice, including changes in pitch, pace, and volume, deepen our understanding of the nonverbal signals that shape our emotional landscape. These vocal cues weave complexity and subtlety into the fabric of communication, offering a richer, more nuanced view of others' feelings and intentions. Mastery in reading these signals not only enhances empathetic understanding but also enriches the quality of our interactions, fostering connections that resonate with authenticity and depth.

Interpreting Verbal Cues

While non-verbal cues provide a rich source of emotional insight, the nuances of verbal communication are equally significant. The choice of words, the topics broached, and the stories shared offer glimpses into the emotional undercurrents that shape an individual's experiences and perceptions. Listening, genuinely listening, involves tuning into these verbal cues with keen awareness, discerning not just the content but the emotions that underlie the spoken words. It is in this attentive listening that the subtleties of verbal cues reveal themselves, from the hesitance that hints at uncertainty to the enthusiasm that speaks of passion and interest. This attentive engagement with verbal communication, when practiced with intention, not only deepens understanding but also validates others' emotions and experiences, creating a space where genuine emotional exchange can flourish.

Practice Exercises

The development of proficiency in reading emotional cues, both verbal and nonverbal, requires deliberate practice and a commitment to honing this skill through focused exercises. One such exercise involves observing interactions in a public setting, such as a café or park, where the dynamics of body language and facial expressions can be studied in a natural context. This practice, approached with discretion and respect for privacy, enables the analysis of non-verbal cues in real time, fostering an intuitive understanding of their meanings and implications.

Engaging in active listening exercises, where the focus is placed on truly hearing and understanding the speaker without the intent to respond immediately, offers another avenue for practice. This exercise, which can be undertaken in everyday conversations, encourages a deep engagement with verbal cues, fostering an attentiveness that is both rare and deeply valued. By suspending the urge to formulate responses, we open ourselves to the full spectrum of the speaker's emotions, enhancing our capacity to connect and empathize.

Cultural Considerations

In exploring emotional cues, it's crucial to consider the impact of cultural context. Cultural norms and values profoundly influence how emotions are expressed and interpreted, shaping both verbal and non-verbal communication. What is considered appropriate in terms of facial expressions, gestures, and conversation topics varies widely across cultures, highlighting the need for cultural sensitivity when reading emotional cues. This awareness, rooted in an understanding of and respect for cultural differences, ensures that our interpretations are informed and nuanced, helping us avoid misinterpretation and misunderstanding.

Developing the ability to recognize subtle shifts in facial expressions and to understand the emotional undertones of spoken words requires both practice and a genuine curiosity about others' emotional experiences. This skill not only enriches our interactions but also fosters a deep sense of connection and understanding, bridging the gaps that words alone cannot fill. In this endeavor, we become adept communicators and compassionate listeners, attuned to the unspoken emotions at the core of human connection.

Understanding emotional cues necessitates careful consideration of cultural influences. For instance, in some cultures, direct eye contact is a sign of respect, while in others, it may be seen as confrontational. Similarly, certain gestures or facial expressions that convey specific emotions in one culture may be interpreted differently in another. To navigate these cross-cultural differences effectively, it's essential to approach emotional cues with cultural sensitivity. One strategy is to actively observe and learn about emotional norms and expressions in diverse cultures. This may involve seeking guidance from individuals familiar with specific cultural practices or conducting research to gain insights into the nuances of emotional communication across different cultural contexts. Furthermore, fostering open communication and genuine interest in understanding the emotional perspectives of individuals from diverse cultural backgrounds can help build mutual respect and bridge potential gaps in interpretation. By acknowledging and respecting the myriad ways in which emotions are expressed and interpreted, we can cultivate a more inclusive and empathetic approach to reading emotional cues across cultures.

Empathy in the Digital Age: Connecting Authentically Online

In an era where keystrokes carry the weight of words and screens serve as windows to the soul, the digital landscape presents a paradox of connection; boundless in reach, yet often constrained in depth. The challenge of expressing and interpreting empathy through digital platforms is a testament to this paradox, a reflection of the nuanced dance between authenticity and anonymity that defines online interactions. As we navigate this terrain, the limitations inherent in digital communication demand not only our attention but also our creativity, compelling us to reimagine how empathy can be conveyed across the ether.

In written communication, it's often helpful to acknowledge and validate the emotions of the person you're interacting with. Try phrases like, "I can see how that situation might be really frustrating for you," or "It sounds like you're feeling overwhelmed. Let me know how I can support you." Simple language adjustments can effectively communicate empathy.

Another way to convey empathy is through the strategic use of emojis or punctuation, which can soften the tone of written messages. For instance, a simple smiling emoji or a "thank you!" with an exclamation mark can make a message feel warmer. Just be mindful of cultural differences in how emojis are interpreted to avoid misunderstandings.

The essence of empathy, with its roots deeply embedded in the soil of human experience, thrives on the nuances of facial expression, tone of voice, and body language; elements often diluted or absent in digital exchanges. The flatness of text, devoid of the warmth of a voice or the immediacy of a shared glance, poses a significant barrier to the transmission of empathy, rendering nuanced emotional states difficult to convey and easy to misinterpret. This challenge is further compounded by the asynchronous nature of many online interactions, where the immediacy of response, a key component of empathetic exchange, is replaced by a lag that can dilute emotional intensity and lead to misunderstandings.

In response to these challenges, cultivating digital empathy emerges as a critical skill, requiring both intention and innovation. Tips for conveying empathy in online interactions begin with mindful language and with choosing words that reflect a genuine attempt to understand and validate others' feelings. Phrases that acknowledge the emotional content of a message, such as "It sounds like you're feeling..." or "I can imagine that must be difficult," serve as textual bridges, narrowing the emotional distance between sender and receiver. Additionally, the strategic use of emojis and punctuation can inject a measure of warmth and humanity into digital exchanges, serving as visual cues that approximate the non-verbal signals so integral to empathetic communication.

The role of empathy in building supportive and positive online communities cannot be overstated. In forums, social media groups, and other virtual gathering places, empathy acts as a cohesive force, fostering an environment of mutual respect and understanding. Moderators and members alike play a pivotal role in cultivating this ethos by modeling empathetic behavior in their interactions and encouraging a culture of kindness and support. This collective effort not only enriches the quality of dialogue within these communities but also creates a sanctuary where individuals feel seen, heard, and valued, despite the physical distances that separate them.

Navigating misunderstandings and conflicts in digital communication with empathy and understanding requires a nuanced approach, one that recognizes the limitations of the medium while seeking to transcend them. When misunderstandings arise, as they inevitably will, the impulse to respond defensively is tempered by an empathetic perspective that seeks clarity over victory. Asking for clarification, expressing a willingness to understand the other's viewpoint, and offering one's own perspective with openness and vulnerability can transform potential conflicts into opportunities for deeper connection. This process, though at times painstaking, reinforces the community's fabric, weaving threads of trust and mutual respect that strengthen its resilience.

In this digital age, where connections are forged with clicks and conversations unfold in pixels, the quest for authentic empathy is both challenged and vital. It is a quest that calls for creativity, intention, and a commitment to understanding the human heart, even when it beats on the other side of a screen. As we navigate this terrain, let us hold fast to the tenet that empathy, in all its forms, remains the bridge that connects us, a bridge that spans distances, transcends technology, and reminds us of the shared humanity that unites us all.

The Role of Empathy
in Conflict Resolution

In the intricate web of human relationships, conflicts invariably arise, their roots often entangled in a complex mesh of misunderstood intentions and unmet needs. Within this context, empathy emerges not merely as a balm. Still, as a potent mediator, its application transforms the nature of disputes and guides the involved parties toward a resolution that acknowledges and addresses each party's core concerns. This transformative power of empathy, when wielded with skill and sincerity, can unravel even the most stubborn knots of contention, revealing pathways to understanding and reconciliation that were previously obscured.

Empathy as a Mediator

The role of empathy in mediating conflicts extends beyond the simple recognition of another's emotional state. It entails active engagement with the other's perspective and an immersion in their emotional world, allowing for a nuanced understanding of the motivations and fears driving their stance. This deep dive into the emotional undercurrents of a dispute illuminates the often-overlooked needs and vulnerabilities that fuel conflict, providing a foundation for solutions. When parties in conflict experience genuine empathy, the defensive barriers erected in the heat of disagreement begin to dissolve, giving way to mutual recognition of shared humanity. This subtle yet profound shift paves the way for dialogue and negotiation that prioritize mutual benefit over victory, fostering an environment where resolutions are crafted not at the expense of all involved but for their enrichment.

Listening for Understanding

Central to the mediation of conflicts through empathy is the practice of empathic listening, a mode of engagement that prioritizes understanding over rebuttal. This form of listening demands a suspension of judgment, a setting aside of one's own perspectives and prejudices to fully absorb the narrative of the other. In the throes of conflict, where the instinct to defend and counter often prevails, empathic listening offers a pause, a deliberate slowing of the discourse that allows for the exploration of the emotional and psychological landscapes from which the conflict arises. Such listening is not passive but an active, dynamic process that seeks to uncover the layers of meaning beneath the spoken words. By fostering a space where each party feels heard and validated, empathic listening lays the groundwork for resolutions that reflect a deep engagement with the concerns and aspirations of all involved.

Empathic Negotiation Techniques

Building on the foundation laid by empathic listening, empathic negotiation techniques offer strategic approaches to navigating conflicts with sensitivity and insight. These techniques hinge on recognizing empathy as a reciprocal process, in which the acknowledgment of the other's emotions and needs is met with a willingness to share one's own. In practice, these negotiations may involve articulating one's viewpoint in a way that is both honest and vulnerable, inviting the other party to engage with the conflict not as adversaries but as collaborators seeking a solution. Key to this approach is the framing of needs and desires in non-confrontational language, the use of "I" statements that express personal feelings without attributing blame or intent to the other. By carefully navigating the emotional terrain of conflict, empathic negotiation fosters an atmosphere of trust and openness where creative solutions can flourish.

Case Studies

The power of empathy in resolving conflicts is vividly illustrated in a diverse array of case studies that span both personal and professional realms. In one instance, a long-standing feud between two co-workers, rooted in miscommunication and competition, was diffused through a series of empathic listening sessions. Facilitated by a neutral third party, these sessions allowed each individual to express their grievances and aspirations without fear of reprisal. This led to a newfound understanding of the other's perspective and a joint commitment to cooperation. Another case involved a family torn by strife following the division of an estate, where empathy-based mediation helped bridge the chasm of resentment and misunderstanding. By creating a space where each family member could voice their emotions and concerns, the mediation process uncovered underlying issues of recognition and respect, leading to a settlement that honored the emotional and material needs of all parties.

Take, for example, a remote team leader who starts virtual meetings with a brief discussion on team members' current challenges. By encouraging everyone to share personal updates for a few minutes, the leader nurtures a sense of connection and demonstrates empathy in a digital setting. This approach has proven effective in strengthening team bonds despite the lack of face-to-face interaction.

Similarly, consider an online mental health support community where moderators model empathetic responses to posts. They acknowledge members' experiences through validation and thoughtful reflections, fostering a supportive, compassionate environment. This community encourages members to share openly, reinforcing the power of empathy in creating a safe space, even online.

These cases, though distinct in their details, share a common thread: the recognition of empathy as a transformative force in conflict resolution. Through the practices of empathic listening and negotiation, conflicts that once seemed insurmountable are approached with a new lens, one that values connection and understanding over division and discord. Therefore, empathy transcends its role as a mere supplement to conflict-resolution tactics, becoming a cornerstone and guiding force that shapes and enhances how we navigate the unavoidable conflicts woven into the intricate fabric of human relations.

Strategies for Overcoming Digital Communication Challenges

Mindful Pausing Before Responding

Before responding to a message, especially in emotionally charged situations, take a moment to reflect on the emotions behind it. Ask yourself, "What is this person feeling, and how can I acknowledge that in my response?" This pause allows you to consider the most empathetic way to respond, minimizing misunderstandings.

Ask Clarifying Questions

When communicating online, avoid making assumptions about the other person's emotions. Instead, ask clarifying questions like, "Can you tell me a bit more about what's been going on? I want to make sure I understand." This invites more open dialogue and can prevent miscommunication.

Empathy in Resolving Online Conflicts

Conflict Resolution Techniques for Digital Communication

When resolving conflicts in digital interactions, start by acknowledging your own emotional state. Use "I feel" statements, such as, "I feel concerned about how we're communicating right now." This simple technique can prevent escalation by reducing defensiveness. Then, reframe responses to clarify intent, like, "My intention is not to dismiss your experience, but rather to understand it more fully."

Empathetic Listening

Practicing reflective listening can also be powerful online. Take the time to re-read the other person's message to fully capture its emotional nuances. Before replying, try rephrasing their points to ensure you've understood them correctly. This reflective practice can minimize misunderstandings and show a genuine commitment to understanding.

Cultivating Compassion: Beyond Empathy

In the intricate mosaic of human emotion and connection, compassion emerges as the transcendent layer that extends beyond merely understanding others' feelings. It embodies an active, fervent drive to alleviate others' suffering, transforming empathy into action. Distinguishing between empathy and compassion is akin to differentiating between acknowledging the storm clouds and actively providing shelter from the rain. Compassion, therefore, is empathy in motion; a dynamic force propelling us towards alleviating the discomforts and sorrows of those around us.

The pathway to fostering compassion involves a series of exercises that not only heighten our sensitivity to others' distress but also amplify our inclination towards benevolent action. Among these, loving-kindness meditation stands as a beacon, guiding individuals through visualization and mantra repetition to cultivate feelings of unconditional positive regard for self and others. This practice begins with the self, for compassion flows freely only when we acknowledge and address our own suffering. It then radiates outward, extending warm wishes of happiness, health, and peace to loved ones, acquaintances, and even those with whom we have conflicts, dissolving barriers of resentment and indifference as it broadens.

Volunteering represents another potent avenue for cultivating compassion, offering tangible opportunities to witness and alleviate others' struggles. Engaging in acts of service, whether in local communities or through digital platforms, not only provides immediate relief to those in need but also deepens our understanding of the vast and varied landscapes of human suffering. This direct engagement with others' hardships fosters a profound sense of connection and shared humanity, reinforcing the imperative of compassion in our interactions and endeavors.

The benefits of nurturing compassion extend far beyond the immediate alleviation of others' suffering, enriching the fabric of our personal and collective existence. On an individual level, the practice of compassion has been linked to enhanced mental and physical well-being, a byproduct of the deep sense of fulfillment and interconnectedness it engenders. Societally, compassion acts as a unifying force, bridging divides and fostering an environment of cooperation and mutual respect. In a world often marred by conflict and division, compassion stands as a testament to the potential for kindness and understanding to transcend boundaries and heal wounds.

Incorporating compassion into the minutiae of daily life necessitates a shift in perspective, a conscious decision to view each interaction through the lens of kindness and generosity. This can be as simple as offering a word of encouragement to a struggling colleague or as profound as dedicating one's efforts to causes that address systemic sources of suffering. The essence lies in recognizing every moment as an opportunity to extend compassion and to choose actions that reflect our deepest values of empathy and care. Integrating compassion into our everyday habits and exchanges not only enhances our personal experiences but also plays a crucial role in nurturing a wider ethos of empathy, comprehension, and proactive engagement.

As we navigate the complexities of fostering compassion in a world that often seems predisposed to indifference and hostility, let us hold fast to the belief in the transformative power of kindness. Let us remember that each act of compassion, no matter how small, contributes to a collective tide of change, a movement towards a world where understanding, care, and action coalesce to create a reality grounded in empathy and united in purpose. In this pursuit, compassion emerges not as an abstract ideal but as a tangible practice, a choice we make day by day, moment by moment, to reach beyond ourselves and touch the lives of others.

In conclusion, the journey to cultivate compassion is one marked by intention, practice, and a steadfast commitment to translating empathy into action. Through practices like loving-kindness meditation and volunteering, we not only deepen our understanding of others' suffering but also take meaningful steps to alleviate it. The benefits of this endeavor ripple outwards, enhancing our own well-being and enriching our communities with a spirit of generosity and mutual respect. As we move forward, integrating compassion into the fabric of our daily lives, we lay the foundation for a more empathetic, connected world, one act of kindness at a time.

Chapter Summary: Developing Empathy: The Unseen Bridge

Introduction to Empathy

- Empathy, a fundamental component of emotional intelligence, allows us to perceive and resonate with others' emotional states. This chapter explores empathy as a skill that transcends innate traits, emphasizing its role in fostering deep, genuine connections and enhancing both personal and professional relationships. Developing empathy enables us to navigate the complexities of human interaction with greater understanding and compassion.

Walking in Their Shoes: Practical Empathy-Building Exercises

- **Empathy as a Skill**: Empathy involves both cognitive and emotional components. Cognitive empathy provides an intellectual understanding of another's perspective, while emotional empathy enables us to feel what they feel. Together, they form a comprehensive approach to connecting with others.
- **Role-Playing Scenarios**: These exercises allow individuals to experience situations from someone else's perspective, fostering understanding. For example, a workplace role-

playing activity where employees step into each other's roles can build appreciation and respect among team members.

- **Empathy Circles**: In small group settings, participants share personal stories while others listen attentively. This practice, which focuses on understanding rather than problem-solving, breaks down barriers and emphasizes our shared humanity.
- **Daily Empathy Challenges**: Simple tasks, like engaging with someone from a different background or expressing gratitude, help cultivate an empathetic mindset. Over time, these challenges build empathy, enhancing everyday interactions.

Reading Emotional Cues: Verbal and Non-Verbal Communication

- **Non-Verbal Cues**: Facial expressions, body language, and vocal tone reveal emotions that words alone might not convey. For instance, a smile can signify warmth, while crossed arms might suggest discomfort. Mastering the art of interpreting these cues enhances our empathetic understanding and connection with others.
- **Verbal Cues**: Language choice, topic emphasis, and storytelling provide insight into emotional states. Practicing active listening, which focuses on understanding the speaker without interrupting, allows us to discern the emotional layers in conversations, validating the other's experiences and emotions.
- **Practice Exercises**: Observing people in public settings and focusing on non-verbal cues helps refine this skill. Additionally, active listening exercises, in which we withhold immediate responses, foster deeper engagement with verbal cues and facilitate genuine empathy.
- **Cultural Considerations**: Understanding that cultural norms shape emotional expression is vital for accurately reading cues. Awareness of these differences ensures that our interpretations remain respectful and informed, helping avoid misunderstandings and promoting cross-cultural empathy.

Empathy in the Digital Age: Connecting Authentically Online

- Digital communication, while vast in reach, often lacks the depth of face-to-face interactions. The absence of visual and tonal cues compounds the challenge of conveying empathy online. Nonetheless, digital empathy can be cultivated through mindful language use, such as validating emotions with phrases like "It sounds like you're feeling…," and using emojis to soften and humanize messages.
- **Building Supportive Online Communities**: Empathy is crucial in creating positive virtual spaces. By modeling empathy and encouraging respectful dialogue, online communities can foster environments of mutual respect and understanding, making members feel valued despite physical separation.
- **Navigating Conflicts Online**: Misunderstandings are common in digital exchanges. Approaching these situations with empathy, seeking clarification, and expressing openness to others' viewpoints can transform conflicts into opportunities for deeper connection.

The Role of Empathy in Conflict Resolution

- **Empathy as a Mediator**: Empathy helps us understand others' perspectives during conflicts, facilitating resolutions that prioritize mutual respect and benefit. When both parties feel genuinely heard, defensive barriers dissolve, paving the way for solutions rooted in understanding rather than division.
- **Listening for Understanding**: Empathetic listening requires setting aside personal biases to engage fully with the other's story. This approach fosters a deeper understanding of underlying needs and motivations, which are essential for productive conflict resolution.
- **Empathic Negotiation Techniques**: Using non-confrontational language and "I" statements helps frame

needs constructively, encouraging open, honest communication. Through empathic negotiation, parties work collaboratively towards resolutions that reflect shared values and respect.

Cultivating Compassion: Beyond Empathy

- **From Empathy to Compassion**: Compassion extends empathy into action, driving us to alleviate others' suffering. While empathy involves understanding, compassion is the desire to help. This chapter outlines ways to cultivate compassion, such as loving-kindness meditation, which promotes positive regard for oneself and others.
- **Volunteering and Acts of Service**: Engaging in service deepens our awareness of shared humanity and offers tangible ways to mitigate suffering. These experiences foster a sense of connection, reinforcing the importance of compassion in daily life.
- **Integrating Compassion into Daily Life**: Acts of kindness, whether simple gestures or substantial commitments, enrich our experiences and contribute to a more empathetic society. By choosing compassion, we create a ripple effect that extends beyond ourselves, uniting us in purpose and understanding.

Conclusion

Developing empathy and compassion not only enhances our relationships but also enriches our lives. Through exercises, digital engagement, conflict resolution, and acts of service, empathy becomes a bridge to deeper connections, transforming our interactions and communities. This chapter emphasizes empathy's role as a cornerstone of emotional intelligence and a guiding principle for authentic, meaningful relationships in an increasingly complex world.

FIVE

EFFECTIVE COMMUNICATION SKILLS

Picture yourself at a dinner table, the tantalizing scent of freshly cooked pasta wafting through the air. Across from you, a friend shares a story. You're not just hearing the words; you're fully engaged, nodding along, your spoon forgotten above your plate. This moment is the essence of active listening; a skill that, when mastered, can deepen connections, foster empathy, and unlock understanding on levels you never thought possible. In these seemingly ordinary exchanges, the true power of hearing and comprehending another's words is revealed, opening the door to connection, warmth, and personal growth in every conversation.

Active Listening: The Key to True Understanding

Principles of Active Listening

Active listening is more than just hearing words; it's about fully engaging with the speaker's message, both verbal and non-verbal. The key pillars of this skill are giving undivided attention to the speaker, showing a genuine interest in their message, and providing feedback that acknowledges understanding. This form of listening creates a respectful, open communication environment where speakers feel valued, and listeners gain deeper insights into the speaker's thoughts and feelings. The power of feedback in this process cannot be overstated. It's the tool that enlightens us, informs our responses, and helps us feel more confident in our ability to communicate effectively.

Active Listening Techniques: Mirroring and Summarizing

Mirroring involves reflecting the speaker's body language and verbal cues, subtly signaling that you are fully present and engaged. This technique, when used thoughtfully, fosters a sense of rapport and connection. Summarizing, on the other hand, entails paraphrasing the speaker's message back to them to ensure clarity and understanding. It acts as a bridge, confirming that the message transmitted is the message received, and often uncovers nuances or emotions that may have been overlooked.

Imagine, for instance, a scenario where a colleague is sharing concerns about an upcoming project deadline. Employing active listening, you mirror their concern through your body language; leaning in slightly, maintaining eye contact; and then summarize their main points, saying, "So, what I'm hearing is that you're feeling overwhelmed by the timeline and unsure about the resources available." This approach not only validates their feelings but also encourages a more open dialogue, making the example more vivid and relatable for the reader.

Barriers to Active Listening

Several common obstacles can hinder active listening, from internal distractions like personal thoughts to external interruptions such as noise. Recognizing and addressing these barriers is crucial for effective communication. It requires determination and commitment. For instance, turning off notifications on your phone during conversations can signal to the speaker that they have your full attention, thereby enhancing the quality of the exchange.

Practicing Active Listening: Exercises to Enhance Skills

Engaging in active listening exercises can significantly improve this skill and boost your confidence in conversations. One practical method involves pairing with a partner to share stories or discuss topics of mutual interest, with one person speaking while the other practices active listening techniques. Afterward, the listener summarizes the speaker's message, and the roles are then reversed. This exercise, repeated regularly, sharpens your ability to listen actively, understand fully, and develop more meaningful connections, motivating you to practice consistently.

Another effective exercise is the 'reflection session,' where, at the end of the day, you reflect on the conversations you've had and evaluate your listening performance. Consider the moments when you felt most engaged and those when your attention waned, exploring the reasons behind these fluctuations. This self-reflection fosters an awareness of your listening habits and highlights areas for improvement. For instance, you can ask yourself questions like 'Did I maintain eye contact during the conversation?' or 'Did I interrupt the speaker at any point?' This exercise can help you identify specific areas where you can improve your active listening skills.

Active listening, with its emphasis on fully engaging with the speaker and understanding their message, stands as a testament to the power of communication to bridge gaps, deepen connections, and foster empathy. By practicing and refining this skill, we unlock the potential for richer, more meaningful interactions, strengthening relationships, and expanding our understanding of the world around us. Embracing emotional honesty and vulnerability in listening can inspire trust and openness, making interactions more genuine and impactful.

Assertiveness Training: Speaking Your Truth Respectfully

In the complex world of interpersonal communication, where expressions, emotions, and expectations merge, assertiveness stands out as a crucial skill. It skillfully navigates the middle ground between passivity and aggression, serving as a key component in effective conversation. Assertiveness, in its essence, embodies the practice of expressing one's thoughts, feelings, and needs in a manner that is direct yet respectful, an artful negotiation between self-advocacy and empathy. The cultivation of this skill not only enriches the individual's palette of communication strategies but also enhances the overall quality of interactions, fostering environments where clarity, respect, and mutual understanding flourish.

The demarcation between assertiveness and aggressiveness, often blurred in the heat of conversation, merits a closer examination. Assertiveness operates on a foundation of confidence and respect, recognizing one's rights and needs alongside those of others. It seeks a harmony in which voices, regardless of volume, find a space to be heard and acknowledged. Aggressiveness, by contrast, bulldozes this balance, prioritizing one's desires at the expense of others, often leaving a trail of resentment and misunderstanding in its wake. The subtle yet profound distinction underscores the transformative potential of assertive communication. It paves the way for constructive rather than divisive interactions, empowering individuals to navigate conversations with confidence and respect.

The strategies for nurturing assertiveness are as diverse as the individuals who seek to embrace this skill. Among these, the practice of using 'I' statements stands out as a cornerstone technique, a linguistic shift that places the speaker's experience at the forefront without casting blame or judgment. This approach, 'I feel frustrated when meetings start late,' versus 'You're always late to meetings,' encapsulates the assertive ethos, offering a perspective that is personal yet non-confrontational. Additionally, the technique of 'fogging,' which involves accepting any truth in criticism without self-deprecation or defensiveness, exemplifies an assertive stance, navigating criticism with grace and poise.

Role-playing exercises, a dynamic method for honing assertiveness, facilitate a safe exploration of this skill within controlled settings. These simulations, ranging from scripted scenarios to impromptu interactions, offer participants a platform to practice assertive communication, experiment with various techniques, and receive real-time constructive feedback. The value of these exercises extends beyond the mechanics of dialogue, delving into the nuances of tone, body language, and emotional regulation, elements that are integral to assertive expression. Envision, for instance, a role-play centered on requesting a deadline extension. This exercise not only sharpens verbal assertiveness but also cultivates an awareness of the non-verbal cues that accompany such requests.

As individuals embark on the path of assertiveness training, they encounter a landscape rich with opportunities for personal growth and improved communication. The journey, marked by moments of introspection, experimentation, and adaptation, reveals the profound impact of assertiveness on the quality of one's interactions and relationships. Seen through the prism of assertiveness, dialogues become conduits of empathy, pathways where the rich mosaic of human emotions and experiences is recognized and valued. In this light, assertiveness training emerges not merely as a skill development endeavor but as a profound engagement with the art of communication, an exploration of the delicate balance between expressing oneself and honoring the other.

The Language of Emotion: Expressing Feelings Constructively

In the intricate dance of interpersonal relations, the ability to articulate emotions with clarity and honesty is a vital pillar, supporting the weight of our most cherished connections. This delicate endeavor, wherein we strive to convey the depth and breadth of our feelings without casting shadows of blame or accusation, navigates the fine line between vulnerability and assertiveness. It beckons us to delve into the realm of emotional expression to uncover the tools and techniques that enable us to share our inner worlds with both courage and consideration.

I-Statements and Emotional Honesty

At the heart of constructive emotional communication lies the practice of utilizing I-statements. This linguistic strategy focuses on the speaker's feelings rather than attributing causality or intent to the listener. This approach shifts the narrative from one that potentially incites defensiveness to a dialogue grounded in personal experience and perception. For instance, saying, "I feel disconnected when we don't spend time together," rather than "You never make time for us," invites a response rooted in understanding rather than rebuttal. It opens the door to a space where emotions are not battlegrounds but bridges, facilitating connections that thrive on empathy and mutual respect.

The essence of I-statements extends beyond mere sentence structure; it encapsulates a commitment to emotional honesty, a willingness to own one's feelings and share them with authenticity. This level of openness requires not just linguistic adjustment but a deeper attunement to one's emotional landscape, an awareness of the nuances of one's feelings, and the contexts that give them shape. It challenges us to peel back the layers of our emotional armor to reveal the raw, unvarnished truth of our experiences, trusting that our vulnerability will be met with understanding.

Overcoming Fear of Emotional Expression

Yet, for many, the path to such openness is fraught with apprehension. The fear of emotional expression, whether borne of past rejections or the anticipation that vulnerability will be mishandled, looms large, casting long shadows over our capacity for connection. To navigate this terrain, where the fear of exposure clashes with the desire for authenticity, requires a measured approach, one that acknowledges these fears while gently pushing against their boundaries.

Strategies for overcoming these barriers often begin with small steps, incremental shifts that gradually build one's confidence in sharing emotions. Initiating conversations about less contentious feelings or in more private settings can serve as a preliminary exercise, a way to test the waters of emotional expression without the immediate risk of overwhelming exposure. This gradual exposure, coupled with the reinforcement of positive experiences of being heard and understood, lays the groundwork for more significant leaps for conversations that delve into the heart of one's emotional world with both bravery and finesse.

Moreover, the cultivation of a supportive environment, one that cherishes openness and cultivates trust, plays a crucial role in mitigating the fear associated with emotional expression. Surrounding oneself with individuals who value and practice emotional honesty creates a buffer against the anxieties that accompany vulnerability, offering a safe space where feelings can be shared without the specter of judgment or dismissal. It is within these environments that the fear of emotional expression finds its antidote in the shared understanding and mutual respect that flourish in the presence of authenticity.

Practical Exercise

To hone the skill of expressing emotions constructively, engaging in practical exercises that simulate real-life scenarios proves invaluable. One such exercise involves the drafting of emotional scripts, written dialogues that articulate one's feelings, needs, and desires using I-statements. This practice, which can be undertaken independently or with a trusted confidant, allows exploration of language and structure for conveying emotions, providing a template that can be adapted for live conversations. Through this process, individuals not only refine their ability to communicate emotions effectively but also deepen their understanding of their emotional needs and how best to articulate them.

Another exercise centers on role-playing, where participants alternate between expressing emotions and responding to them within a framework that emphasizes active listening and empathy. This reciprocal engagement, which mirrors the dynamics of real-world interactions, offers insights into the challenges and rewards of emotional communication, highlighting the impact of language, tone, and body language on the conveyance of feelings. It serves as a crucible in which the fears and barriers to emotional expression are both confronted and transcended, paving the way for a mode of communication that is both authentic and constructive.

The journey toward mastering the language of emotion, toward navigating the complexities of expressing feelings constructively, is both challenging and rewarding. It demands a commitment to self-awareness, courage in the face of vulnerability, and a steadfast dedication to cultivating relationships grounded in honesty and empathy. Through the adoption of I-statements, the gradual overcoming of fears, and engagement in practical exercises, this journey unfolds, leading us to a place where emotions are not just spoken but truly heard, where connections are not just maintained but deepened. In this endeavor, we find not just the means to express ourselves but the path to a richer, more connected existence, where the language of emotion speaks of understanding, compassion, and the indelible bonds that tie us to one another.

Feedback: Giving and Receiving with Grace

In the nuanced theater of human interaction, feedback stands as a pivotal scene, one where growth and understanding are the protagonists, yet vulnerability and misinterpretation lurk as potential antagonists. This complex interplay, rich with opportunities for personal development and bond strengthening, invites exploration of the mechanics of constructive, empathetic feedback. It beckons a closer look at the threads that weave the fabric of effective feedback, unraveling the skills necessary to give and receive such insights with poise and openness.

The act of conveying feedback, a gesture aimed at nurturing growth or refining dynamics, necessitates a delicate balance. It demands a straightforward approach that ensures the message is understood as intended, yet is suffused with empathy, acknowledging the recipient's perspective and emotional state. The artistry involved in this endeavor mirrors that of a sculptor, where each chisel stroke is deliberate, aimed at revealing the form within the marble without fracturing its essence. Herein lies the challenge: to sculpt without harming, to illuminate areas for growth while preserving dignity and respect.

Techniques that facilitate the delivery of constructive feedback have deep roots in the principles of respect and clarity. Sandwiching, a method in which feedback is framed with positive comments, serves to cushion the impact of critiques, making the pill of criticism easier to swallow. Yet, its effectiveness hinges on the authenticity of the praise; disingenuous compliments can tarnish the trust upon which effective feedback rests. A more direct approach, presenting critiques as observations rather than judgments and coupled with suggestions for improvement, fosters an environment where feedback is not a verdict but a roadmap for development. This method, transparent in its intentions, nurtures a dialogue in which growth is the collective aim and understanding paves the way.

On the flip side of this coin is the art of receiving feedback, a performance requiring grace and an openness to self-reflection. The initial impulse to defend or deflect, a natural response to perceived criticism, must be tempered by recognizing feedback as a gift, albeit one that might not always be wrapped in the most appealing package. The strategies to embrace this gift gracefully involve a pause, a moment of introspection where the feedback is considered from a stance of curiosity rather than defensiveness. Questions like "What truth can I find in this?" or "How can this insight serve my growth?" transform the experience of receiving feedback from endurance to enlightenment. This shift in perspective, from feedback as an assault on competence to input as a beacon guiding improvement, alters not just the reception but the trajectory of personal and professional growth.

Envisioning scenarios that offer practice in the dual arts of giving and receiving feedback illuminates paths toward proficiency. Workshops or group settings, where participants engage in role-plays focused on feedback exchange, provide fertile ground for honing these skills. Within these constructs, individuals can experiment with techniques, explore the emotional landscapes that feedback traverses, and receive immediate, constructive feedback on their feedback. These exercises, reflective of real-world dynamics yet removed from the stakes of personal and professional relationships, serve as laboratories for growth. Participants emerge not only with sharper skills but also with a heightened awareness of the complexities and potential of feedback.

In these practices, a culture where feedback is both given and received as an act of respect and a vehicle for growth begins to take root. It fosters relationships where honesty is encased in empathy, where critiques are not roadblocks but signposts on the journey toward excellence. Through this culture's lens, feedback transcends its traditional role, becoming a dialogue where learning and understanding are the ultimate goals.

In this exploration of feedback, from its delivery to its reception, a map unfolds, one that guides through the intricacies of constructive criticism and the reception of such with openness. It paints a picture in which feedback, nuanced and layered, becomes a cornerstone of interpersonal dynamics, a tool for refining skills and deepening connections. This landscape, rich with the possibilities of growth and understanding, invites an engagement with feedback that is both thoughtful and intentional, transforming potential points of contention into opportunities for development and insight.

Navigating Difficult Conversations: A Step-by-Step Guide

In the labyrinth of human communication, specific dialogues stand as formidable challenges, their potential for conflict and misunderstanding as vast as their capacity for growth and resolution. The art of navigating these conversations with tact and empathy is akin to walking a tightrope, where each word must be measured, and every emotion carefully managed to maintain balance and progress. This section explores the tools and strategies needed to navigate this tightrope, transforming daunting exchanges into opportunities for understanding and connection.

Preparing for Difficult Conversations

The groundwork for any challenging dialogue begins long before words are exchanged. Preparation, a crucial yet often overlooked component, involves a deep dive into one's intentions, expectations, and desired outcomes. This reflective process demands honesty and clarity, urging individuals to confront not only what they wish to convey but also what they hope to achieve through the exchange. Setting clear intentions serves as a compass, guiding the conversation and ensuring it remains anchored to the core issues at hand.

Additionally, anticipating potential responses and emotional reactions can illuminate paths through the conversation, identifying strategies to maintain engagement and empathy even in the face of resistance or high emotion. This preparatory stage is also an opportune time to cultivate a mindset of openness and curiosity, a stance that encourages flexibility and adaptability as the dialogue unfolds.

Communication Techniques for Difficult Conversations

Once the foundation is laid, the focus shifts to executing the conversation, where specific communication techniques become invaluable tools for navigating the complexities of human emotion and response. Techniques such as reflective listening, which involves echoing the speaker's words to demonstrate understanding and validation, and framing questions to encourage exploration rather than defensiveness, are pivotal. These methods not only facilitate deeper understanding but also foster a dialogue atmosphere in which all parties feel heard and respected.

Another significant technique lies in the strategic use of silence. Far from passive, silence offers a powerful means of allowing emotions to settle and giving space for reflection, both for the speaker and the listener. It is in these pauses that insights often emerge, revealing underlying issues or concerns that may not have been apparent amidst the continuous flow of dialogue.

Managing Emotions

The emotional terrain of difficult conversations is fraught with potential pitfalls, where unmanaged feelings can derail discussions and lead to outcomes far from the intended goals. Strategies for managing one's emotions, therefore, are as critical as the words spoken. This management involves recognizing the physical and psychological signals of emotional escalation and employing techniques such as deep breathing or pausing the conversation to prevent overwhelm.

Simultaneously, the ability to respond to others' emotions with empathy and validation becomes a bridge across tumultuous waters, easing tensions and fostering a mutual respect and understanding. This dual focus on managing both personal and others' emotions underscores the complex interplay of self-awareness and empathy required to navigate challenging dialogues successfully.

Case Studies

The theoretical frameworks and strategies discussed gain depth and dimension through the lens of real-world applications, as illustrated in a series of case studies. One such study involves a workplace conflict between two departments over resource allocation, a situation fraught with tension and competing interests. Through active preparation, reflective listening, and a concerted effort to manage emotions, the parties involved reached a mutually beneficial agreement, transforming a potential source of ongoing discord into an opportunity for collaboration and understanding.

Another case recounts a family navigating the emotional minefield of estate planning, a process often laden with complex feelings and historical dynamics. The deliberate use of communication techniques designed to promote openness and empathy, coupled with a focus on managing emotions, allowed the family to address sensitive issues with compassion and respect, ultimately strengthening familial bonds rather than eroding them.

These case studies, and others like them, serve as tangible evidence of the power of emotional intelligence in reshaping difficult conversations, highlighting the potential for growth, understanding, and resolution inherent in every challenging dialogue.

In traversing the landscape of difficult conversations, from the initial steps of preparation to the nuanced management of emotions and the strategic application of communication techniques, we uncover not only the potential for conflict but also the immense possibilities for connection and growth. This journey, though fraught with challenges, offers a testament to the transformative power of empathy, understanding, and skillful communication in navigating the complexities of human interaction. As we move forward, these principles guide us not just in difficult dialogues but across the broader spectrum of our relationships and interactions, illuminating paths toward more profound connection and mutual understanding.

Chapter Summary: Effective Communication Skills

Introduction to Active Listening

- Effective communication begins with active listening, a skill that goes beyond merely hearing words to engage with the speaker's message fully. Through principles like giving undivided attention and showing genuine interest, active listening creates a space where both parties feel valued and understood. This chapter explores active listening's power to deepen connections and foster empathy, ultimately enhancing all relationships.

Active Listening Techniques

- **Mirroring and Summarizing**: Mirroring subtly reflects the speaker's body language and verbal cues, building rapport. Summarizing or paraphrasing the speaker's message back ensures clarity and demonstrates understanding. For example, when a colleague shares concerns about a deadline, summarizing with, "So, you're feeling overwhelmed by the timeline," validates their feelings and encourages further discussion.
- **Barriers to Active Listening**: Distractions, both internal (like wandering thoughts) and external (such as phone notifications), can disrupt listening. Recognizing these barriers and taking steps to mitigate them, such as silencing notifications, can improve communication quality.
- **Exercises for Improvement**: Practicing active listening, such as partner discussions in which one person speaks, and the other listens and summarizes, enhances this skill over time. Reflection sessions at the end of the day, evaluating moments of effective and ineffective listening, also highlight areas for improvement.

Assertiveness Training: Respectful Expression

- Assertiveness is the balance between passivity and aggression, allowing for self-expression that respects both one's own needs and those of others. Distinct from aggressiveness, assertiveness emphasizes confidence without overpowering others, creating constructive interactions that foster mutual respect and understanding.
- **Techniques for Assertiveness**:
    - **Using "I" Statements**: This technique frames thoughts and feelings from a personal perspective, such as "I feel frustrated when meetings start late," to avoid blaming others and maintain a non-confrontational tone.
    - **Role-Playing Exercises**: Practicing assertive communication through role-playing scenarios, like requesting a deadline extension, helps build confidence and refine body language, tone, and emotional control in a supportive environment.

The Language of Emotion: Expressing Feelings Constructively

- Articulating emotions with clarity and honesty is essential for authentic connection. This process uses **I-statements** to express feelings constructively and without blame, opening a dialogue that emphasizes empathy and understanding.
- **Overcoming Barriers**: Fear of vulnerability often prevents emotional expression. Starting with smaller disclosures and surrounding oneself with supportive individuals can gradually build confidence. Drafting emotional scripts and role-playing with trusted friends also provide practical ways to practice this skill.

Feedback: Giving and Receiving with Grace

- Feedback is crucial for growth, yet it requires a delicate balance to be both constructive and empathetic. Techniques like **sandwiching feedback** (framing criticism between positive comments) make difficult messages easier to accept. Using observations instead of judgments helps maintain a respectful, non-accusatory tone.
- **Receiving Feedback**: Embracing feedback with openness and curiosity, rather than defensiveness, allows for self-improvement. Reflecting on questions like, "What can I learn from this?" transforms feedback into a learning opportunity. Practice exchanges, such as workshops or role-plays, can help refine the skills for both giving and receiving feedback effectively.

Navigating Difficult Conversations

- Difficult conversations often require preparation, including reflecting on intentions and potential responses. Setting a clear purpose ensures that discussions remain focused and productive, while anticipating possible reactions can help maintain composure and empathy.
- **Communication Techniques**: Techniques like reflective listening and strategic silence can help manage emotions and foster understanding. Pausing to let emotions settle and contemplate responses contributes to a balanced, effective exchange.

Case Studies and Real-World Applications

- The chapter illustrates these principles through real-life examples, such as resolving workplace conflicts and family disputes, showcasing how active listening, assertiveness, emotional expression, and empathetic feedback can transform challenging interactions into opportunities for growth and understanding.

Conclusion

Mastering practical communication skills, such as active listening, assertiveness, emotional expression, constructive feedback, and navigating difficult conversations, enriches personal and professional relationships. Through these skills, we cultivate deeper connections, empathy, and a capacity to handle complex interactions with grace and insight, transforming communication into a pathway for personal growth and stronger, more fulfilling relationships.

SIX

BUILDING AND MAINTAINING STRONG RELATIONSHIPS

In the silent spaces between words spoken during a heartfelt apology, where the hum of vulnerability resonates more profoundly than the verbal admission of wrong, trust begins its delicate dance of reconstruction. It's in these moments when two individuals sit across from each other, the air thick with anticipation and the weight of past grievances, that the true essence of trust reveals itself; not as a grandiose gesture but as a series of small, consistent actions that, brick by brick, rebuild the shattered edifice of a once-sturdy relationship.

Trust, then, is not merely a component of strong relationships; it is the very mortar that binds them, providing the strength and resilience to withstand the trials and tribulations inherent in human connection. Whether in the realm of personal intimacy or the dynamics of a professional team, trust transforms interactions, elevating them from mere exchanges to profound connections that foster growth, understanding, and mutual respect.

Trust Building: The Foundation of Every Relationship

The Importance of Trust

In relationships, trust operates on multiple levels, from confidence in a partner's fidelity to assurance in a friend's confidentiality. This multifaceted nature underscores its role as a foundational element, without which the architecture of a relationship becomes unstable and susceptible to the erosive forces of doubt and insecurity. Trust, therefore, is not an optional luxury but a necessity, the absence of which renders relationships shallow and transient.

Steps to Building Trust

Building trust is an endeavor that requires intentionality and effort, a commitment to actions that convey reliability, honesty, and vulnerability. Consider the act of keeping promises, no matter how small, from returning a borrowed book to being punctual for meetings. These seemingly inconsequential actions are potent demonstrations of reliability, signaling to others that their expectations and needs are respected and valued.

Transparency, too, plays a pivotal role in fostering trust. In situations where mistakes are made or misunderstandings arise, the willingness to openly acknowledge these errors, without defensiveness or obfuscation, speaks volumes about one's integrity. It's akin to allowing someone a glimpse into the inner workings of a timepiece, revealing its complexities and imperfections, thereby engendering a deeper appreciation and understanding.

Vulnerability, often perceived as a risk, is the linchpin in the trust-building process. It involves the courage to share one's fears, hopes, and insecurities, inviting others into one's emotional world. This act of openness, far from being a display of weakness, is a testament to strength, an invitation for others to engage in a relationship with honesty and depth.

Rebuilding Trust

The path to mending trust, once fractured, is arduous yet not insurmountable. It begins with acknowledging the hurt caused and a sincere apology that seeks not to excuse but to understand the impact of one's actions. This acknowledgment, coupled with a commitment to change, lays the groundwork for the slow process of healing.

Forgiveness, a critical step in this journey, requires a willingness to release resentment, not as an endorsement of the transgression but as a liberation from its emotional shackles. This release paves the way for open, honest communication, where discussions about fears, boundaries, and expectations can occur, fostering an environment where trust can gradually be restored. It's important to note that forgiveness is a process, not an event. It may take time and effort, but it's a necessary part of rebuilding trust. It's about letting go of the hurt and anger, not necessarily forgetting what happened or excusing the behavior.

The Process of Forgiveness and the Role of Vulnerability in Rebuilding Trust

Rebuilding trust after it's been broken requires more than just an apology; it's a multifaceted process rooted in forgiveness, vulnerability, and a commitment to growth. Understanding the steps involved in forgiveness can help both parties move forward and establish a stronger foundation of trust.

Embracing Vulnerability

For both the person seeking forgiveness and the one granting it, vulnerability is essential. It requires an openness that goes beyond simply acknowledging fault; it involves sharing emotions honestly and allowing oneself to be truly seen. Vulnerability is critical when discussing the hurt caused, as it invites genuine empathy and deepens the emotional connection. For instance, a person who has been hurt may need to openly express their feelings of betrayal or disappointment, while the other must listen without becoming defensive or dismissive.

Steps to Forgiveness

Forgiveness is a journey rather than an immediate event. Here are some key steps that can facilitate the process:

1. **Acknowledge the Impact**: The person who caused harm should begin by understanding the full extent of the hurt they've caused. This means listening attentively to the other person's perspective and recognizing the emotional toll their actions have.
2. **Commit to Personal Change**: Rebuilding trust involves a sincere commitment to personal growth. This might include adopting new habits, improving communication skills, or seeking professional guidance to ensure that past mistakes are not repeated.
3. **Release Resentment**: For the person who was hurt, letting go of resentment can be challenging but essential to the process. This step isn't about excusing the behavior but rather about freeing oneself from lingering bitterness. Practicing self-compassion and focusing on one's well-being can help release the hold that anger or hurt may have.
4. **Reaffirm Boundaries**: Establishing clear boundaries helps prevent future misunderstandings and reinforces mutual respect. Reaffirming these boundaries with a trusted friend, partner, or colleague demonstrates a commitment to maintaining a safe and supportive relationship moving forward.

Vulnerability as a Pathway to Healing

Vulnerability strengthens the bond between individuals by allowing them to communicate openly about their fears and insecurities. For example, sharing anxieties about the relationship's future or expressing a need for reassurance fosters mutual understanding. When both parties engage at this level of openness, they build a foundation of authenticity and trust. Practicing vulnerability may feel uncomfortable initially, but it ultimately allows for a more honest and compassionate connection.

Trust-Building Exercises

Trust-building, whether in the initial stages or as part of a restoration effort, benefits from structured exercises that encourage vulnerability and empathy. An exercise such as sharing personal stories of fear or triumph, focusing on the emotions experienced, allows participants to connect on a deeper level, fostering empathy and understanding. Similarly, collaborative challenges, where success is contingent on mutual support and reliability, serve as practical demonstrations of trustworthiness and teamwork. Other exercises could include role-playing scenarios that require trust and communication or engaging in a shared hobby or activity that fosters a sense of connection and mutual understanding.

In the professional realm, trust exercises might involve team members sharing constructive feedback in a circle, where each person, in turn, expresses appreciation for a colleague's contribution and offers suggestions for growth. This exercise, conducted in a spirit of respect and support, reinforces the team's bonds of trust, highlighting the value of each member's input and the collective commitment to improvement.

In conclusion, trust stands as the cornerstone of strong, enduring relationships, its presence a testament to the depth and authenticity of human connection. Through intentional actions that demonstrate reliability, honesty, and vulnerability, trust is built and maintained, serving as the foundation for meaningful relationships. Whether in the realm of personal intimacy or professional teamwork, cultivating trust transforms interactions, elevating them from mere exchanges to profound connections that foster growth, understanding, and mutual respect.

Setting Healthy Boundaries: The Balance Between Closeness and Personal Space

In the intricate dance of human relationships, the delineation of boundaries serves as the unspoken choreography that ensures each participant moves with respect and awareness of the other's space. This delicate equilibrium between closeness and personal autonomy is not innate; it is cultivated with intention and understanding, shaping interactions that are both enriching and respectful. At the heart of this cultivation lies the recognition of boundaries as the silent sentinels of our emotional, physical, and psychological well-being, guardians that empower us to interact with openness and trust.

Understanding Boundaries

Boundaries, in their essence, are the demarcations of our comfort zones, invisible lines that define how we allow others to treat us and how we engage with the world. These are not barriers erected out of fear or mistrust but rather statements of self-respect and self-awareness. They signal to others how we wish to be treated, what we are willing to tolerate, and where we draw the line on behaviors that encroach upon our sense of self and well-being. In acknowledging the significance of boundaries, we recognize our worth and affirm that our needs, feelings, and comfort hold value and merit consideration. Boundaries are not just about saying 'no' to things that make us uncomfortable; they're also about saying 'yes' to things that make us feel safe and respected. They're about setting the tone for how we want to be treated in our relationships, and they're a key part of building and maintaining trust.

Identifying Personal Boundaries

The task of pinpointing one's personal boundaries demands introspection, a deep dive into the self that explores the terrains of past experiences, core values, and non-negotiables. This exploration is not a passive reflection but an active engagement with one's most profound truths, unearthing the standards by which we govern our interactions. It might begin with recognizing moments of discomfort or resentment in past interactions, signals that boundaries were either nonexistent or transgressed. From these insights, a clearer picture emerges, one that outlines the parameters within which we feel respected, heard, and valued.

Communicating these boundaries to others is the bridge that transforms internal clarity into external harmony. This communication is not a declaration of ultimatums but a sharing of personal truths delivered with honesty and respect. It involves clear, direct expression, free from ambiguity, that leaves little room for misinterpretation. For instance, articulating the need for solitude to recharge without apology or excessive explanation sets a clear boundary around personal space and time.

Respecting Others' Boundaries

Just as we seek understanding and respect for our boundaries, so too must we extend that courtesy to others. Respecting another's boundaries is a testament to our empathy and consideration, an acknowledgment of their autonomy and preferences. This respect often requires active listening, an attentiveness to verbal and non-verbal cues that indicate where their boundaries lie. It also demands flexibility and the willingness to adapt our behaviors and expectations to recognize their comfort zones. In doing so, we foster relationships built on mutual respect and understanding, where each individual feels valued and heard.

The act of respecting boundaries is not a one-time adjustment but a continuous process, a dance of give-and-take that evolves with the relationship. It is underpinned by open dialogue, where discussions about boundaries and needs are not shunned but welcomed as opportunities for deeper connection and understanding.

Boundary Setting Exercises

Cultivating the skill to set and maintain healthy boundaries benefits from practical exercises that simulate real-life scenarios. Role-playing, for instance, offers a dynamic platform for practicing boundary communication. In these scripted interactions, individuals can experiment with different ways to assert their boundaries and navigate potential pushback with calmness and assertiveness. Feedback from these sessions provides invaluable insights into the effectiveness of various approaches, refining the ability to establish boundaries with confidence.

Another exercise involves journaling, a reflective practice where individuals can articulate their experiences with boundary setting, noting what felt effective and what did not. This written record becomes a tool for growth, highlighting patterns and areas for improvement. It also serves as a reminder of the progress made, reinforcing the importance and value of healthy boundaries in cultivating strong, respectful relationships.

In setting boundaries, we navigate the delicate balance between closeness and personal autonomy, ensuring that our interactions are both enriching and respectful. This process, rooted in self-awareness and mutual consideration, shapes the foundation of relationships that thrive on honesty, respect, and understanding. Through practical exercises and continuous dialogue, we hone our ability to delineate and communicate our boundaries, fostering connections that honor the worth and well-being of all involved.

The Dynamics of Teamwork: EI in Professional Settings

At the core of any thriving organization lies a network of teams, each pulsating with the collective aspirations and endeavors of its members. The fabric of these teams is woven not just from the threads of individual competencies but significantly from the emotional intelligence (EI) that permeates their interactions. The nuanced interplay of empathy, self-awareness, and emotional regulation within these groups often dictates the rhythm of their success or the discord of their challenges. It is within this intricate dance of individual emotions and collective goals that the true essence of teamwork in professional settings reveals itself.

Fostering a team environment ripe for the growth of emotional intelligence starts with a conscious shift in perspective, acknowledging the significant contributions that emotionally intelligent actions make to the organizational fabric. This recognition paves the way for strategies that nurture these behaviors, transforming the workplace into a crucible for emotional growth and collaboration. Among these strategies, team-building exercises emerge as potent tools, not merely as activities to fill a scheduled slot in corporate retreats but as deliberate efforts to foster empathy, enhance communication, and build a resilient foundation of trust and mutual respect.

Incorporating team-building exercises that focus on empathy involves creating scenarios in which team members step into each other's roles, confronting the challenges and pressures their colleagues face daily. This experiential learning not only broadens their understanding of each other's roles but also cultivates deep-seated empathy, recognizing the emotional landscapes navigated by their peers. Similarly, exercises that simulate high-pressure situations, requiring teams to collaborate under constraints, highlight the critical role of emotional regulation and collective efficacy in navigating stress.

Promoting open communication practices within teams is another cornerstone of enhancing emotional intelligence. This promotion involves establishing channels and norms that encourage the expression of thoughts and feelings in a respectful, constructive manner. Regular check-ins, where team members share not only updates on their tasks but also their emotional state, can demystify the often invisible emotional dynamics that influence team performance. Such practices underscore the importance of listening with empathy, responding with understanding, and engaging in dialogues that bridge differences and foster a sense of belonging.

Addressing emotional conflicts within teams, an inevitable aspect of any collaborative endeavor, requires a nuanced approach, one that leverages emotional intelligence to transform potential discord into opportunities for growth. When conflicts arise, the emphasis on empathetic listening and validating each member's feelings becomes paramount. Conflict resolution sessions that prioritize understanding the underlying emotional triggers and needs pave the way for solutions that are not merely acceptable to all parties but also enrich the team's emotional resilience.

The profound influence of elevated emotional intelligence on team performance is highlighted through a rich collection of case studies. One such study recounts the journey of a project team within a tech company, initially plagued by miscommunication and frustration. The introduction of structured team-building exercises focused on empathy and emotional regulation led to a remarkable turnaround. Team members, now equipped with a deeper understanding of each other's emotional and professional landscapes, collaborated with renewed vigor and creativity, catapulting the project to success ahead of its deadline.

Another case study delves into the dynamics of a healthcare team in which the high-stress environment had eroded trust and cooperation. Through workshops designed to enhance emotional literacy and open communication practices, the team discovered new ways to express concerns and support one another. This newfound emotional intelligence fostered a sense of unity and shared purpose, significantly improving patient care and team satisfaction.

These narratives, each unique in its context and challenges, converge on a singular truth: the profound influence of emotional intelligence in shaping the dynamics of teamwork. In professional settings where the confluence of diverse personalities, skills, and emotions can either catalyze success or precipitate discord, the deliberate cultivation of emotional intelligence becomes not just beneficial but essential. It transforms workplaces into environments where empathy, understanding, and emotional resilience are not lofty ideals but lived realities, where teams not only achieve their objectives but also embark on a journey of emotional growth and mutual respect.

Rekindling Connections: Repairing Strained Relationships

In the quiet aftermath of discord, where the echoes of harsh words and the shadows of misdeeds linger, the prospect of mending frayed bonds looms like a daunting precipice. Within this challenging situation, there's a chance not just to heal the frayed edges but to rebuild the fabric of our relationships stronger than before, integrating a newfound resilience through understanding, forgiveness, and a rejuvenated dedication to trust. The path to revitalization, while fraught with vulnerability, demands a navigation that is both deliberate and empathetic. This process begins with illuminating strains and their origins.

Recognizing Relationship Strains

The initial step toward healing is acknowledging the rift itself, a task that requires mindfulness to discern subtle shifts in dynamics. These unspoken tensions belie deeper issues. These strains manifest in myriad ways, from the frostiness of communication to the evasion of shared spaces, each a symptom of underlying discontent. Beneath this surface lie the roots, often entangled in unmet expectations, unhealed hurts, or unacknowledged grievances, factors that, left unaddressed, widen the chasm between individuals. The act of recognition, therefore, is not merely an observation but an invitation to delve into the complexities of the relationship to confront the discomforts that have led to estrangement.

Steps to Repair Relationships

With recognition comes the choice to mend, a decision that sets into motion a series of actions aimed at bridging divides. The initial overture, often the most challenging, involves reaching out, an act imbued with humility and the willingness to broach the chasms of silence. Following this outreach, the articulation of an apology, a genuine expression of remorse for hurts caused, intentionally or not, serves as a balm to wounded spirits. This apology, to be effective, must transcend mere words, embodying a depth of sincerity that acknowledges the pain inflicted and the role played in the discord.

Forgiveness, the counterpart to apology, is the next beacon along the path to reconciliation. It is a release, not just of the transgressor but of the aggrieved, from the bondage of resentment. This step, possibly the most arduous, demands a magnanimity of spirit, a choice to liberate the relationship from the shackles of past misdeeds, paving the way for the re-establishment of trust. Trust, in this context, is not unquestioningly reinstated but gradually rebuilt through actions that validate the sincerity of apologies and the depth of commitment to change.

The process of rebuilding is iterative, marked by small, consistent acts that demonstrate reliability, respect, and reinvigorated affection. It is in these acts, the sharing of vulnerabilities, the demonstration of support, the commitment to shared goals, that trust finds fertile ground to flourish anew.

Maintaining Rekindled Relationships

The restoration of a relationship marks not an end but a beginning, the initiation of a phase where the focus shifts from healing to growth. Maintenance, in this phase, hinges on the continuous cultivation of open communication, the bedrock upon which trust and understanding steadily grow. It involves not just the sharing of thoughts and feelings but the active engagement with those of the other, fostering an environment where honesty flourishes and vulnerabilities are safeguarded.

Equally vital is the commitment to mutual growth, a shared journey that embraces not just the aspirations of each individual but those of the relationship itself. This commitment manifests in a willingness to explore new experiences, to support each other's endeavors, and to confront, together, the challenges that arise, using them as catalysts for deepening the bonds of connection.

Adaptability, too, plays a crucial role, recognizing that relationships, like the individuals within them, are dynamic. The capacity to navigate change, recalibrate expectations, and renegotiate boundaries ensures that the relationship remains resilient and able to evolve in harmony with the shifting landscapes of life.

Personal Stories

Embedded within the narrative of rekindling are the stories of those who have traversed the rugged terrain of reconciliation, each tale a testament to the potency of empathy, forgiveness, and enduring affection. One such story unfolds in the lives of Alex and Jordan, whose partnership, marred by betrayal, found its way back to trust through a painstaking process of open dialogue, therapy, and a mutual determination to start anew. Their journey, marked by setbacks and victories, illuminates the path to forgiveness and showcases the transformative power of understanding and commitment.

Another narrative chronicles the journey of a fractured family, where longstanding grievances and misunderstandings had erected walls of estrangement. The decision to engage in family counseling, to lay bare each member's hurts and hopes, paved the way for healing. Through sessions marked by tears and laughter, the family discovered not just the roots of their discord but the unbreakable ties of love that bound them, leading to a renewed sense of kinship and shared joy.

These stories, and countless others unspoken, serve as beacons of hope, exemplifying the possibility of renewal in the aftermath of strife. They underscore the resilience of the human spirit, the capacity for change, and the enduring power of love to heal and transform relationships, knitting together once more the threads of connection that bind us.

Emotional Intelligence in Love: Strengthening Couple Dynamics

Within the intimate weave of romantic partnerships, emotional intelligence (EI) emerges as a pivotal thread, coloring interactions with the hues of empathy, understanding, and attuned communication. This subtle yet profound faculty enhances not only the depth and resilience of love but also its capacity to evolve and thrive amidst the ebbs and flows of shared life experiences. The essence of EI in the context of love transcends mere emotion management; it embodies the ability to navigate the intricate dance of two distinct emotional landscapes, merging them into a harmonious tableau that celebrates both unity and individuality.

The infusion of EI into the heart of romantic relationships transforms the quality of connection, enriching the soil in which love grows with nutrients of mutual respect, deep listening, and the shared language of authentic emotional expression. This transformation is most visible in the realm of communication, where the principles of EI guide partners to engage in dialogues that bridge differences and illuminate common ground. Enhanced communication in love, therefore, is not merely about articulating thoughts and desires but about creating a sacred space where vulnerabilities are honored and understanding flourishes. It involves active listening that seeks to comprehend not just words but the emotions that animate them, responding with empathy that validates and connects.

Addressing the inevitable challenges and conflicts that emerge in the complex fabric of a relationship requires a strong application of emotional intelligence. The capacity to recognize and regulate one's emotional responses, and to approach conflicts with a mindset geared toward resolution and growth, marks the difference between discord and harmony. Strategies rooted in EI, such as pausing to reflect before responding in anger or practicing empathy to understand a partner's perspective, become invaluable tools in transforming conflict from a source of division to a catalyst for deeper understanding and intimacy. This approach fosters a dynamic where challenges are met with cooperation and compassion, reinforcing the bonds of love with each resolved conflict.

The journey towards strengthening love through EI is marked by deliberate practices that cultivate these emotional skills within the relational context. Exercises designed to enhance emotional awareness and empathy, such as sharing personal emotional histories or engaging in role-reversal scenarios, enrich partners' understanding of each other's emotional worlds. Regular check-ins, where each partner shares their current emotional state and listens to the other's with genuine interest and empathy, foster a continuous connection that nurtures the relationship's emotional health. These practices, simple in their execution yet profound in their impact, weave EI into the daily rhythm of a relationship, ensuring that love is not only expressed but deeply felt and understood.

As couples navigate the complexities of their shared journey, the application of EI becomes a beacon that guides them towards a love that is resilient, fulfilling, and ever-deepening. It underscores the recognition that love, in its most authentic form, is not just a feeling but an act of continuous emotional attunement and understanding. It heralds a paradigm in which relationships are not merely endured but cherished as avenues for mutual growth, healing, and joy.

In this light, the cultivation of emotional intelligence in romantic love emerges not as an optional enhancement but as a vital component of healthy, lasting partnerships. It represents a commitment not only to nurturing love but also to elevating it, ensuring it remains a source of strength, comfort, and inspiration. Through the lens of EI, love transcends mere affection, embodying a profound connection that celebrates the full spectrum of human emotion.

As we transition from exploring the nuances of emotional intelligence within the intimate weave of romantic relationships, we are reminded of EI's transformative power across all realms of human interaction. The principles of empathy, understanding, and attuned communication that enrich romantic partnerships are equally applicable in the broader scope of our social and professional lives. In embracing EI as a guiding philosophy, we open ourselves to deeper connections, enriched interactions, and an enhanced capacity for compassion and understanding. This journey through the landscape of EI, from the personal to the interpersonal, invites us to reflect on the myriad ways in which emotional intelligence shapes our world, offering a vision of a future where empathy and understanding are not just valued but embodied in our daily lives.

The Role of Adaptability in Relationship Resilience

As relationships evolve, so too must the dynamics between those involved. Over time, changes in personal goals, life circumstances, or external factors can influence how individuals relate to one another. Adaptability, therefore, becomes essential in navigating these shifts, enabling partners, friends, or colleagues to recalibrate their expectations and realign their connection with the relationship's current needs.

Navigating Change Together

When faced with change, emotionally intelligent relationships allow for flexibility and understanding. A fundamental part of this is maintaining open communication about evolving needs and preferences. Rather than viewing changes as threats, seeing them as opportunities for growth allows both parties to bring fresh perspectives and renewed energy into the relationship.

Consider, for example, a friendship that started in college but now faces the realities of different career paths and family obligations. By practicing adaptability, both friends can acknowledge the shift in circumstances and find new ways to connect, such as scheduling regular calls or planning annual meet-ups. These efforts demonstrate an understanding that while the friendship may look different, it remains valuable and worth nurturing.

Renegotiating Boundaries

Boundaries are not static; they change as individuals grow and their priorities shift. Adaptable relationships are built on the recognition that boundaries may need to be redefined over time to reflect new life phases or individual development. For instance, a couple that starts a family may need to set new boundaries around personal time to ensure they can meet their new responsibilities while also honoring their need for individual space.

In navigating these adjustments, it is helpful to discuss openly what each person needs to feel supported. This practice of renegotiating boundaries enables individuals to respect each other's evolving needs, fostering mutual understanding and flexibility.

Practical Steps to Enhance Adaptability

To strengthen adaptability in relationships, consider the following practices:

- **Embrace Change with Curiosity**: Approach shifts in the relationship with an open mind, focusing on learning from new experiences rather than resisting them.
- **Regular Check-ins**: Schedule times to discuss how each person feels about the direction of the relationship. These check-ins provide a platform for expressing new needs and exploring ways to adjust to changes together.
- **Flexibility in Expectations**: As individuals grow, their roles and contributions to the relationship may shift. Embrace these changes and align expectations with current realities rather than holding onto past dynamics.

By cultivating adaptability, relationships can remain resilient and fulfilling, growing stronger as they adjust to life's inevitable changes.

Chapter Summary: Building and Maintaining Strong Relationships

The Role of Trust in Relationships

- Trust serves as the cornerstone of all meaningful relationships, whether in personal or professional settings. It's built on small, consistent actions that signal reliability, honesty, and vulnerability. Trust not only provides the foundation for enduring connections but also fosters environments where growth and mutual respect can flourish.

Steps to Building Trust

1. **Consistency and Reliability**: Simple acts like keeping promises and being punctual signal respect for others' time and needs, laying the groundwork for a trusting relationship.
2. **Transparency**: Acknowledging mistakes openly, without defensiveness, builds credibility and strengthens trust.
3. **Vulnerability**: Sharing fears and insecurities with others encourages a deeper level of connection. This openness, far from being a weakness, reinforces trust by inviting honesty and emotional depth.

Rebuilding Trust

- When trust is broken, mending it requires a sincere apology, a commitment to change, and a focus on open communication. Forgiveness plays a crucial role in this process, allowing both parties to let go of resentment. Over time, trust is restored through actions that consistently demonstrate accountability and respect.

Trust-Building Exercises

- Exercises like sharing personal stories and engaging in collaborative tasks enhance empathy and reinforce trust. In professional settings, activities such as team circles, where members share feedback in a respectful environment, build camaraderie and reinforce collective commitment to growth.

Setting Healthy Boundaries

- Boundaries define personal comfort zones and ensure respectful interactions. They are not barriers but rather expressions of self-respect and self-awareness, allowing individuals to engage with others while honoring their own needs.

Identifying and Communicating Boundaries

- **Self-Reflection**: Recognize past moments of discomfort as indicators of necessary boundaries. This reflection clarifies personal values and non-negotiables.
- **Clear Communication**: Express boundaries directly and respectfully, for instance, by stating a need for personal time without apology or excessive explanation.
- **Respecting Others' Boundaries**: Listening actively and adapting behaviors in response to others' boundaries fosters mutual respect. Continuous dialogue keeps boundaries in sync with evolving relationships.

Boundary Setting Exercises

- Role-playing exercises and journaling can help individuals practice setting and maintaining boundaries. These activities offer practical tools for refining boundary communication skills and reinforcing personal comfort zones in relationships.

The Importance of Emotional Intelligence (EI) in Teamwork

- EI is essential for successful teamwork, as it impacts communication, empathy, and emotional regulation. Teams with high EI foster environments where trust, understanding, and resilience can thrive, allowing members to work cohesively and effectively.

Developing EI in Teams

- **Team-Building Exercises**: Activities that promote role-reversal or simulate high-pressure scenarios cultivate empathy and emotional regulation. Regular check-ins where members share updates and emotional states create open lines of communication.
- **Conflict Resolution**: Addressing conflicts with empathic listening and validating emotions turns potential discord into opportunities for team growth. Understanding emotional triggers and needs leads to more harmonious, practical solutions.

Case Studies

- Examples from the workplace show how EI transformed team dynamics, such as a tech team improving communication through empathy-focused exercises or a healthcare team enhancing cooperation with emotional literacy training.

Rekindling Connections: Repairing Strained Relationships

- Acknowledging strained relationships and choosing to mend them opens the door for forgiveness and renewed trust. This process involves reaching out, offering sincere apologies, and consistently demonstrating change.

Steps to Repair Relationships

1. **Apology and Forgiveness**: A heartfelt apology, combined with a commitment to change, initiates healing. Forgiveness liberates both parties from past grievances, allowing for the re-establishment of trust.
2. **Rebuilding Through Small Actions**: Gradual, consistent actions that convey reliability and care rebuild trust over time.
3. **Maintaining Repaired Relationships**: Continuous communication, adaptability, and a commitment to mutual growth keep relationships strong and resilient.

The Role of EI in Romantic Relationships

- In romantic partnerships, EI enhances communication, fosters empathy, and helps navigate conflicts constructively. It strengthens love by attuning partners to each other's emotions and deepening their connection through shared emotional experiences.

Strengthening Love Through EI

- **Empathy and Attuned Communication**: EI facilitates active listening, where partners engage deeply with each other's feelings and needs, building understanding and reinforcing connection.
- **Navigating Conflicts**: EI strategies, like pausing before reacting or seeking to understand a partner's perspective, transform conflicts into opportunities for growth.
- **Practices for Deeper Connection**: Exercises such as sharing emotional histories and conducting regular emotional check-ins enhance relational intimacy and foster ongoing emotional awareness.

Conclusion

Emotional intelligence weaves through every aspect of building and maintaining strong relationships. By cultivating trust, setting boundaries, developing teamwork, repairing strained bonds, and enhancing romantic relationships, EI helps create meaningful, enduring connections. Whether in personal or professional realms, EI transforms interactions into opportunities for empathy, understanding, and shared growth, enriching the quality of human connection across all facets of life.

SEVEN

EMOTIONAL INTELLIGENCE: LEADING WITH EMPATHY

In a dimly lit conference room, where the hum of a projector fills the air, and the scent of black coffee lingers, a leader stands before their team. The atmosphere is charged, not with anticipation for the quarterly earnings report about to be presented, but with an undercurrent of shared respect and understanding that pervades the space. This scene, seemingly mundane, encapsulates the essence of empathetic leadership; a style that, though subtle in its execution, revolutionizes workplace dynamics and cultivates an environment where trust, collaboration, and innovation flourish.

The Empathetic Leader: A New Paradigm

Empathy as Leadership Strength

Empathy, often misconstrued as mere emotional consolation, finds its true power in leadership, transforming the traditional paradigm. It's not about coddling or avoiding hard truths but understanding the team's emotional landscape, recognizing fears, aspirations, and the silent struggles that may impede progress. This deep understanding fosters a culture of trust and mutual respect, where individuals feel seen and valued, not merely for their output but for their humanity. In such an environment, motivation and commitment naturally surge, not as a response to external incentives but from a genuine connection to the leader's vision and empathy.

Leading by Example

A leader's actions and behaviors set a precedent, crafting the team's ethos and values. When a leader consistently demonstrates emotional intelligence, actively listening, showing genuine concern for team members' well-being, and managing their emotional responses even under stress, they model a standard. This standard, rooted in empathy and self-awareness, becomes the team's guiding principle in moments when deadlines loom and pressure mounts. The team's response mirrors the leader's composure and empathy, fostering a resilient and supportive work environment.

The Empathetic Leadership Style

Characteristics of empathetic leadership extend beyond mere understanding to active engagement with team members' emotional and professional needs. This leadership style is characterized by open lines of communication, where feedback is not only encouraged but valued as a critical insight. Empathetic leaders possess a keen ability to read between the lines, discerning the unsaid concerns and aspirations that influence team dynamics. This insight allows for tailored support that addresses individual and collective needs, thereby enhancing team cohesion and driving performance.

Case Studies

Consider the transformation within a multinational corporation's marketing department, plagued by high turnover and declining morale. The appointment of a new director, known for her empathetic leadership style, marked a turning point. By prioritizing one-on-one meetings, she gained insights into each team member's unique challenges and motivations. This approach led to strategic role adjustments that aligned better with individual strengths and aspirations, resulting in a significant uptick in team performance and job satisfaction. The director's empathy and tailored leadership approach exemplified how understanding and support could revitalize a struggling team.

Another example is a tech startup, where rapid growth has led to fragmented teams and a diluted company culture. The CEO, recognizing the need for a unified vision and stronger team connections, initiated a series of empathy workshops. These workshops, facilitated by experts in emotional intelligence, equipped leaders across the company with the skills to understand and support their teams effectively. The result was a notable improvement in cross-departmental collaboration and a rejuvenation of the company's core values, proving the indispensable role of empathy in navigating the challenges of growth and change.

In these cases, and countless others, the principles of empathetic leadership demonstrate a profound impact on organizational culture and outcomes. Leaders who embrace empathy not only enhance their team's well-being and performance but also inspire a ripple effect that transforms the entire organizational landscape. This new paradigm of leadership, rooted in emotional intelligence and empathetic engagement, heralds a future where workplaces are not just centers of productivity but havens of mutual respect, understanding, and shared purpose. It also sets the stage for a future of work where emotional intelligence and empathy are not just desirable traits but essential skills for leaders and team members alike.

As we delve deeper into the nuances of emotional intelligence in leadership, we uncover a landscape rich with opportunities for growth, innovation, and connection. The journey toward embodying empathetic leadership is both challenging and rewarding, demanding a commitment to self-awareness, continuous learning, and genuine engagement with the emotional dimensions of team dynamics. It's important to note that this journey is not without its challenges. The potential for transformation within leaders, teams, and organizations is immense, promising not just enhanced performance but also a deeper, more meaningful approach to work and collaboration. In this exploration, we find not just the mechanics of leadership but its heart, where empathy and understanding light the way toward a future of possibility and shared success.

Motivating Others: The Role of Emotional Intelligence

In the nuanced domain of leadership, the alchemy of motivation remains one of its most elusive yet transformative elements. The ability to ignite a spark within team members, propelling them not just to fulfill their tasks but to embrace them with a sense of purpose and passion, hinges significantly on the leader's emotional intelligence. This intricate dance of influencing and inspiring others weaves through understanding what drives human behavior, acknowledging the varied emotional landscapes of each team member, and crafting an environment that nurtures continuous engagement and motivation.

Understanding Motivation

Fundamentally, motivation is deeply rooted in the emotional underpinnings that reflect the diverse needs, desires, and goals inherent to each person. While traditional theories of motivation have underscored the significance of external rewards and recognition, the emotional intelligence perspective delves deeper, exploring the emotional aspects that fuel motivation. It recognizes that beyond the tangible incentives lies a realm of emotional needs - the need for belonging, for feeling valued, for achieving mastery, and for autonomy. A leader, through the lens of emotional intelligence, becomes an astute observer, discerning these needs and aligning them with the team's and organization's overarching goals. This alignment, when achieved, transforms mere tasks into missions, imbuing daily routines with a sense of purpose and direction. Understanding and addressing these emotional needs is not just a part of leadership but a necessity for creating a motivated and engaged team.

Personalized Motivation Strategies

The one-size-fits-all approach to motivation, often a default in many leadership playbooks, is being rendered obsolete by emotional intelligence. The recognition that each team member's emotional triggers and needs differ radically calls for a personalized approach to motivation. This strategy considers not just the professional capabilities of an individual but their emotional profile - what excites them, what concerns them, and what aspirations they harbor. For instance, while one team member might find motivation in public recognition, another might find it in opportunities for learning and personal growth. Tailoring motivational strategies, therefore, demands a deep engagement with the team, a commitment to understanding their emotional landscapes, and the creativity to link these insights to motivational tactics that resonate on a personal level.

The Role of Recognition

In the spectrum of motivational strategies, recognition holds a special place. Its power lies not in the grandeur of the gesture but in its relevance and timing. Emotional intelligence informs the effective use of recognition, guiding leaders not just to acknowledge the achievements but to do so in a manner that resonates emotionally with the team member. It transcends the generic 'job well done' to a nuanced acknowledgment that connects with the individual's intrinsic drivers and values. For instance, recognizing a team member's relentless pursuit of excellence in a challenging project in front of peers not only validates their efforts but also reinforces their sense of belonging and worth within the team. This recognition, when aligned with the individual's emotional needs, acts as a potent motivator, fostering a culture of appreciation and continuous effort.

Building a Motivational Environment

Beyond individual interactions and strategies lies the broader canvas of the workplace environment, a space that either stifles motivation or allows it to bloom. Crafting an environment that consistently motivates and engages employees requires a deliberate design, one that embeds emotional intelligence into the very fabric of the organizational culture. This environment champions open communication, where feedback and ideas flow freely, fostering a sense of ownership and belonging among team members. It also emphasizes the importance of psychological safety, a space where taking risks and expressing vulnerabilities is not just accepted but encouraged. Furthermore, it honors the vast array of perspectives and experiences each team member brings, acknowledging diverse backgrounds and viewpoints as integral to the team's collective strength. In such an environment, motivation thrives, fueled by a sense of inclusion, respect, and the genuine connections that bind the team together.

In this complex interplay of understanding motivation, tailoring strategies to individual needs, recognizing achievements meaningfully, and cultivating a motivating environment, emotional intelligence emerges as the critical catalyst. It is the thread that weaves through these strategies, transforming the act of motivating from a managerial task to a leadership art. Through this lens, leaders not only inspire action but also nurture a sense of purpose, belonging, and fulfillment among their team members, driving not just productivity but also a shared commitment to excellence and growth.

Conflict Management: An Emotionally Intelligent Approach

Identifying Emotional Undercurrents

In the labyrinth of human interactions that define the workplace, conflicts, much like storms, are inevitable, yet their resolution hinges on the nuanced understanding of the emotional currents beneath. Leaders, adept in the intricacies of emotional intelligence, learn to navigate these turbulent waters by first recognizing the subtle signs of brewing discontent. This skill involves keen observation, not just of the words spoken but also of the silences between them, the shift in body language, the uncharacteristic hesitations, or the too-quick acquiescence that signals unease. These signals, often overlooked, are the map to the underlying issues fueling conflict. By attuning to these emotional cues, leaders can preemptively address concerns before they escalate, approaching each interaction with a sensitivity that seeks to understand before seeking to be understood. This proactive engagement acts as a balm, soothing tensions and fostering an environment where conflicts, when they arise, are navigated with empathy and insight.

Emotionally Intelligent Negotiation

The art of negotiation, when imbued with emotional intelligence, transforms from a battlefield of competing interests into a dialogue of collaborative problem solving. Leaders skilled in this art approach negotiations not with rigid agendas but with open minds, ready to listen, understand, and adapt. They employ empathy as a tool, striving to see the world through others' eyes and to understand their needs, fears, and aspirations. This approach does not signify capitulation but strength, showcasing a confidence that solutions can be crafted to meet mutual goals. Techniques such as 'mirroring,' where a leader reflects the emotions and language of the other party, serve to validate their feelings and concerns, creating a space of mutual respect from which compromise can emerge. Moreover, emotionally intelligent leaders use 'framing' to shape discussions in a positive light, emphasizing common goals and shared benefits, thereby steering negotiations towards outcomes that benefit all parties.

Preventing Escalation

The adept application of emotional intelligence serves not only in resolving conflicts but, crucially, in preventing their escalation. Leaders, as stewards of team dynamics, employ a variety of strategies to maintain harmony and address issues at their nascent stage. One such approach involves establishing clear communication channels and norms, encouraging team members to voice concerns early and openly. This openness, coupled with a culture that values emotional expression, ensures that grievances are aired before they fester into larger disputes. Additionally, leaders practice 'active emotional labeling,' a technique where they acknowledge and name the emotions at play during conflicts. This acknowledgment acts as a pressure valve, allowing emotions to be expressed and understood, thereby reducing the likelihood of misunderstanding and escalation. Furthermore, regular team-building activities, designed with a focus on emotional intelligence, cultivate a sense of unity and understanding among team members, making it easier to navigate disagreements with empathy and mutual respect.

Case Scenarios

To illustrate the practical application of these principles, consider a product development team facing a deadline with two key members at odds over the project's direction. The leader, recognizing the emotional undercurrents of stress and fear of failure driving the conflict, convenes a meeting not to dictate a solution but to facilitate understanding. Through active listening and emotional labeling, she creates a space where each party can express their concerns without fear of judgment. By reframing the conflict as a shared challenge, she guides the team towards a solution that honors both perspectives, thus preventing escalation and fostering a stronger, more cohesive team dynamic.

Another scenario involves a customer service department grappling with low morale due to an unpopular policy change. The manager, using emotional intelligence, identifies the root of the discontent as a feeling of powerlessness among the staff. Instead of dismissing these emotions, he acknowledges them, expressing genuine understanding and empathy. He then involves the team in brainstorming sessions to find ways to implement the policy that aligns better with their needs and concerns. This approach not only mitigates the conflict but also empowers the team, transforming a potential source of ongoing discord into an opportunity for collaborative problem-solving.

Through these scenarios and countless others that unfold daily in workplaces around the globe, the value of an emotionally intelligent approach to conflict management becomes evident. Leaders who navigate conflicts with empathy, insight, and a genuine desire for resolution can transform potential crises into opportunities for growth, learning, and deeper connection. In doing so, they not only address the immediate challenges at hand but also lay the groundwork for a culture that celebrates emotional intelligence as a vital tool for collaboration and innovation.

Building Emotional Resilience in Teams

In the theater of modern organizational life, where the specter of uncertainty often looms large and the winds of change blow with relentless force, the concept of resilience emerges not merely as a desirable attribute but as a bedrock upon which teams either stand firm or falter. This resilience, a collective capacity to weather storms and adapt to new realities, assumes a critical role, particularly in periods rife with challenges or marked by significant transformations. It is within this context that leadership, characterized by a high quotient of emotional intelligence, becomes instrumental in cultivating and reinforcing team resilience, ensuring they not only endure but thrive amidst adversity.

The Importance of Resilience

At its core, team resilience encompasses more than the mere ability to bounce back from setbacks. It represents a profound collective agility, an ethos of perseverance and adaptability that enables teams to navigate through periods of disruption with grace and emerge on the other side not just intact but invigorated. This resilience is pivotal, for it is within the crucible of challenges that teams discover their true potential, forging bonds that are both deeper and more durable. The cultivation of such resilience, therefore, does not happen in the absence of adversity but rather through its very presence, through the shared experiences of navigating the unpredictable and often tumultuous waters of organizational life.

Strategies for Strengthening Team Resilience

Leaders seeking to fortify their teams' resilience wield a variety of strategies, each rooted in the principles of emotional intelligence. Foremost among these is fostering a culture of transparent communication, where fears, concerns, and vulnerabilities can be shared without fear of judgment. This transparency not only demystifies the challenges at hand but also encourages a collective ownership of both problems and solutions, engendering a sense of unity and purpose.

Moreover, deliberately cultivating a positive team narrative is pivotal to resilience-building. Leaders, through their communication, have the power to shape perceptions and reframe obstacles as opportunities for growth and learning. By consistently highlighting past triumphs over adversity and underscoring the team's inherent strengths and capabilities, leaders can instill confidence and optimism, fueling collective belief in the team's ability to surmount current and future challenges.

Training and development initiatives specifically designed to enhance emotional intelligence and stress management skills further contribute to team resilience. Workshops that equip team members with tools for emotional regulation, empathy, and constructive feedback not only bolster individual resilience but also enhance the team's collective capacity to support one another during periods of stress.

The Role of Supportive Leadership

In the architecture of team resilience, supportive leadership acts as a keystone, holding the structure together with its weight. Leaders who exhibit high levels of emotional intelligence understand that their role extends beyond mere task delegation or performance monitoring. They act as anchors, providing stability and reassurance through their unwavering support and genuine concern for each team member's well-being. This support manifests in various forms, from one-on-one check-ins to assess individual well-being to the provision of resources and workload adjustments when necessary.

Supportive leaders also excel in recognizing and celebrating not just achievements but efforts, especially during times when outcomes may not meet expectations due to factors beyond the team's control. This acknowledgment of effort fosters a culture of persistence and grit, essential components of resilience, encouraging team members to keep striving despite setbacks.

Creating a Culture of Resilience

The ultimate manifestation of a team's resilience is not in isolated acts of perseverance but in cultivating an enduring culture of resilience. This culture, characterized by mutual support, positivity, and adaptability, becomes the very air the team breathes, ingrained in its daily operations and interactions. Leaders play a crucial role in creating and nurturing this culture, modeling resilience through their actions and attitudes, and actively promoting values that support resilience.

Embedding resilience into the team's DNA involves integrating resilience-building activities into regular team routines, such as reflective debriefs following project completions or challenges, during which lessons learned and strategies for improvement are discussed openly. It also involves creating opportunities for team members to contribute to decision-making processes, empowering them with a sense of agency and control, which is vital for resilience.

Moreover, leaders foster a culture of resilience by creating an environment where failure is not shamed but viewed as a valuable learning opportunity. This perspective encourages experimentation and innovation, recognizing that not every attempt will succeed, but every effort contributes to growth.

In the complex, ever-evolving landscape of modern organizations, the ability of teams to remain resilient in the face of adversity is paramount. Through strategies that foster transparent communication, a positive narrative, and mutual support, and by embodying supportive leadership, leaders can fortify their teams' resilience. This resilience, deeply embedded within the team's culture, ensures that teams not only withstand the challenges of the present but are also well-equipped to embrace the opportunities of the future, navigating the unpredictable with confidence and grace.

The Future of Work: Emotional Intelligence as a Key Skill

Evolving Work Environments

In the shifting sands of contemporary work landscapes, where the digital revolution has reshaped the very fabric of organizational life, the significance of emotional intelligence has surged to the forefront. The transformation of these environments, marked by the rise of remote work, agile teams, and the blurring of traditional boundaries, necessitates a recalibration of the skills considered vital to success. Emotional intelligence, with its emphasis on empathy, self-awareness, and adaptability, emerges not merely as an asset but as a critical component of professional competency. This evolution reflects a broader recognition that the challenges of modern workspaces, characterized by rapid change and uncertainty, demand more than technical prowess; they require a profound understanding of human emotions and the ability to navigate complex interpersonal dynamics.

Preparing for the Future

As organizations stand at the cusp of this new era, the imperative to integrate emotional intelligence into the DNA of their training and development initiatives becomes increasingly apparent. This integration involves a multifaceted approach, beginning with a foundational shift in how emotional intelligence is perceived – from a soft skill to a core competency. Training programs, therefore, must evolve beyond traditional modules to incorporate immersive experiences that simulate real-world challenges, encouraging participants to employ emotional intelligence to navigate conflicts, foster teamwork, and lead with empathy. Furthermore, adopting mentoring and coaching practices focused on developing these competencies offers a personalized pathway for growth, enabling leaders and teams to cultivate emotional intelligence through guided reflection and practical application.

Emotional Intelligence and Technology

In the realm of technology, where artificial intelligence and automation continue to redefine roles and processes, the relationship between emotional intelligence and technological proficiency gains new dimensions. As machines take on tasks previously reserved for humans, the unique value of human contributions increasingly centers on emotional and relational skills. This shift underscores the importance of emotional intelligence in managing remote teams, where digital communication tools serve as the primary medium of interaction. The nuances of conveying empathy, building rapport, and maintaining team cohesion, when separated by screens, underscore the critical role of emotional intelligence in bridging the digital divide. Moreover, the development of emotionally intelligent technologies, from AI-driven HR tools to platforms that enhance remote collaboration, reflects a growing acknowledgment of the need to infuse technology with a deeper understanding of human emotions.

Predictions and Trends

Looking to the horizon, the trajectory of emotional intelligence within the workplace points towards a future where these competencies are not just valued but essential for leadership and organizational success. Predictions suggest a growing emphasis on emotional intelligence in recruitment, with organizations seeking candidates who demonstrate high empathy, adaptability, and self-regulation. This trend is likely to extend beyond hiring practices to influence performance evaluations, career advancement opportunities, and leadership development pathways. As organizations grapple with the complexities of global teams, diverse workforces, and the relentless pace of technological change, the ability to navigate these challenges with emotional intelligence will distinguish successful leaders and resilient teams. Furthermore, the integration of emotional intelligence into organizational culture is anticipated to deepen, transforming workplaces into environments that prioritize well-being, foster meaningful connections, and champion emotional growth alongside professional achievement.

In this landscape, where the forces of technology and globalization continuously redraw the contours of work, the mastery of emotional intelligence emerges as a beacon, guiding organizations towards a future defined by more than efficiency and innovation. It heralds a shift towards workplaces that recognize the indelible link between emotional well-being and professional success, where cultivating empathy, resilience, and self-awareness is seen as fundamental to navigating the challenges and opportunities of the future.

As we close this exploration of emotional intelligence's evolving role in the workplace, we're reminded of its profound impact not only on individual careers but on the very essence of organizational life. This journey through the realms of empathy, motivation, conflict management, and resilience illuminates a path towards a future where work is not just a pursuit of professional goals but a canvas for personal and collective growth. The insights gleaned from this exploration serve as a compass, guiding us towards approaching the challenges ahead with a renewed understanding of the importance of emotional intelligence in shaping not just the leaders of tomorrow but the workplaces they will inhabit.

Chapter Summary: Emotional Intelligence: Leading with Empathy

Empathy as a Leadership Strength

- Empathetic leadership shifts the focus from traditional command-and-control to understanding team members' emotional landscapes. This approach fosters an environment of trust, respect, and collaboration, allowing team members to feel valued and understood, which ultimately enhances motivation and commitment.

Leading by Example

- Empathetic leaders model emotional intelligence by actively listening, showing genuine concern, and managing their emotions under stress. By setting this standard, they influence the team's overall demeanor, resilience, and responsiveness, particularly during high-pressure situations.

Empathetic Leadership Characteristics

- Empathetic leaders go beyond surface-level understanding, engaging with their team's deeper needs and aspirations. They encourage open communication and are attuned to unspoken concerns, allowing for tailored support that enhances team cohesion and performance.

Case Studies

- A multinational corporation's marketing department saw improved morale and reduced turnover when a new, empathetic director took over, tailoring roles to individual strengths and fostering a supportive environment.

- A tech startup's CEO implemented empathy workshops to strengthen connections across teams, resulting in improved collaboration and a renewed sense of company culture.

Motivating Through Emotional Intelligence

- Emotional intelligence enables leaders to tap into their team members' intrinsic motivations, recognizing emotional needs beyond external rewards, such as belonging, value, and personal growth. This approach transforms routine tasks into meaningful missions aligned with individual aspirations.

Personalized Motivation Strategies

- Leaders using emotional intelligence avoid a one-size-fits-all approach. Instead, they identify individual triggers and tailor motivational strategies accordingly. For instance, some may be driven by public recognition, while others are motivated by opportunities for skill development.

The Role of Recognition

- Meaningful recognition, when timely and relevant, serves as a potent motivator. Leaders who understand their team members' emotional drivers can deliver recognition that validates efforts, fosters a sense of belonging, and encourages sustained engagement.

Crafting a Motivational Environment

- Emotional intelligence informs the design of a workplace that promotes open communication, psychological safety, and inclusivity. Leaders cultivate an environment where feedback flows freely, team members feel valued, and diverse perspectives are celebrated, fostering collective motivation.

Emotionally Intelligent Conflict Management

- Leaders with emotional intelligence recognize the emotional currents beneath workplace conflicts. They use empathy to understand concerns, prevent escalation, and approach conflicts as opportunities for collaborative problem-solving.

Emotionally Intelligent Negotiation

- Empathetic leaders engage in negotiations with open-mindedness and a willingness to understand the other's perspective. Techniques like mirroring and framing help establish mutual respect and guide negotiations toward positive, win-win outcomes.

Preventing Escalation

- Emotionally intelligent leaders proactively address grievances by establishing clear communication channels and acknowledging emotions before conflicts escalate. Regular team-building activities further enhance understanding, reducing potential conflicts and promoting harmony.

Case Scenarios

- In a product development team facing conflict over project direction, a leader's active listening and reframing turned a potential escalation into a collaborative solution.
- In a customer service department, a manager addressed morale issues by involving the team in policy implementation decisions, thereby empowering the team and resolving underlying discontent.

Building Emotional Resilience in Teams

- Resilience is critical for teams facing adversity, and emotionally intelligent leaders foster resilience by promoting transparency, positive team narratives, and stress-management skills. This collective resilience empowers teams to navigate challenges with agility and adaptability.

Strategies for Strengthening Resilience

- Transparent communication allows team members to share fears and concerns, fostering unity.
- Positive narratives encourage a focus on past successes and team strengths, building confidence.
- Resilience-building workshops equip team members with emotional regulation skills, bolstering collective resilience.

Supportive Leadership for Resilience

- Emotionally intelligent leaders provide stability by regularly checking in on team members, acknowledging efforts, and celebrating resilience. Their support reinforces a culture of persistence, inspiring teams to rise above setbacks.

Creating a Culture of Resilience

- Leaders model resilience and foster a supportive, adaptable environment where failure is viewed as a learning opportunity. Team routines, such as reflective debriefs and collective decision-making, promote resilience as a shared value, helping teams thrive amid challenges.

Emotional Intelligence as a Key Skill for the Future of Work

- As workplaces evolve with technology and remote work, emotional intelligence has become essential. Leaders who prioritize empathy, adaptability, and interpersonal understanding can navigate digital dynamics effectively, promoting cohesion and engagement even in virtual settings.

Preparing for the Future

- Organizations are increasingly integrating emotional intelligence into training and development programs. Leaders and teams learn to navigate complex interpersonal dynamics, essential for success in fast-changing environments.

Emotional Intelligence and Technology

- As automation transforms tasks, human contributions are increasingly defined by emotional and relational skills. Emotional intelligence is key to managing remote teams and ensuring digital interactions remain personal and meaningful.

Trends in Emotional Intelligence

- The future points to a growing emphasis on emotional intelligence in recruitment and development. Successful leaders will embody empathy and adaptability, while resilient teams will thrive in workplaces that prioritize emotional well-being and connection.

Conclusion

Emotional intelligence enhances leadership by cultivating empathy, motivation, conflict resolution, and resilience. As we embrace these skills, work becomes a space for growth and deeper connection, illuminating a path toward a more compassionate and effective future of work.

EIGHT

ENHANCING TEAM DYNAMICS

In a world where the fabric of teams is often stretched thin by the demands of productivity, deadlines, and innovation, the glue that holds these teams together isn't found in the mechanics of their tasks but in the depth of their emotional connections. When teams function like well-oiled machines, it's tempting to attribute their success solely to skill and dedication. However, beneath the surface of every high-performing team lies a network of emotional bonds, intricate and powerful, forged not in the fires of shared tasks but in the warmth of shared experiences and mutual understanding. This unspoken yet palpable web of connections is the lifeblood of effective collaboration, turning groups of individuals into cohesive units capable of transcending the sum of their parts.

Creating Cohesive Teams: The Role of Emotional Awareness

The Foundation of Team Cohesion

In the realm of team dynamics, emotional awareness acts as the cornerstone upon which the pillars of cohesion and collaboration stand. This awareness goes beyond mere recognition of emotions; it involves an attuned understanding of how these emotions influence interactions within the team, affecting everything from decision-making to conflict resolution. Like a gardener who knows that the health of the soil is just as crucial as the seeds sown, leaders who prioritize emotional awareness cultivate an environment where teams can thrive, rooted in empathy and mutual respect. Leaders need to model and actively promote emotional intelligence within their teams, as their actions and attitudes set the tone for the entire group.

Imagine, during a routine project review, a team member's frustration bubbles to the surface, not at the project's status but from the pressure of unspoken personal challenges. A leader attuned to emotional undercurrents can recognize this not as defiance but as a cry for support, transforming a potential conflict into an opportunity for strengthening team bonds.

Building Emotional Bonds

Strategies for fostering these essential bonds focus on creating shared experiences and facilitating open, heartfelt communication. Regular team retreats serve as a powerful tool, removing members from the daily grind and immersing them in activities that emphasize collaboration over competition and empathy over efficiency. During these retreats, team members engage in exercises designed to reveal personal values and aspirations, bridging professional gaps with personal connections.

For instance, a retreat might include a segment where team members share their most significant non-work achievements, offering a glimpse into their lives outside the office and fostering a deeper understanding of one another's strengths, values, and motivations. This approach not only adds a personal dimension to team interactions, transcending mere job titles and tasks, but also underscores the rich array of abilities and backgrounds each member brings to the team.

Emotional Awareness Exercises

To further enhance emotional awareness within teams, specific exercises can be integrated into regular meetings or dedicated workshops. One effective exercise involves 'active listening,' where team members pair up and share a recent work challenge, with the listener focusing solely on understanding and empathizing with the speaker's experience. This simple exercise deepens emotional connections by encouraging team members to see the world through each other's eyes, fostering a culture of empathy and mutual support. By cultivating these qualities, teams can feel more connected and understanding, leading to improved collaboration and decision-making.

Another valuable exercise is the 'emotion wheel' activity, where team members identify and discuss the emotions they frequently experience in the workplace. This activity not only normalizes the discussion of emotions in a professional setting but also provides insights into the team's emotional landscape, enabling leaders to tailor support and interventions more effectively. Additionally, exercises like 'appreciation circles,' where team members express gratitude for each other's contributions, or 'role reversal,' where team members temporarily switch roles to gain a deeper understanding of each other's challenges, can also be effective in enhancing emotional awareness and team cohesion.

Success Stories

Teams that have prioritized emotional awareness often report transformative effects on their dynamics and outcomes. Consider a software development team facing chronic project delays and rising tensions. By implementing regular emotional awareness exercises and fostering open communication about stressors and challenges, the team witnessed a remarkable turnaround. Team members, now more attuned to each other's emotional states and needs, collaborated more effectively, navigating deadlines with a newfound sense of camaraderie and resilience. The result was not only a significant improvement in project timelines but also a reduction in burnout and an increase in job satisfaction. These success stories serve as beacons of hope, inspiring other teams to embark on their own journey towards emotional intelligence and team cohesion.

Similarly, a marketing team struggling with internal competition and siloed efforts embraced emotional awareness as a core component of their strategy. Through workshops focused on empathy-building and shared goal-setting, the team members developed a deeper appreciation for each other's roles and contributions. This shift in perspective dismantled barriers of competition, fostering a culture of collaboration that propelled the team to new heights of creativity and cohesiveness.

While the benefits of emotional awareness and the deliberate cultivation of emotional bonds are clear, it's essential to acknowledge that this transition can be challenging. Some team members may be resistant to discussing emotions in a professional setting, or leaders may struggle to balance the need for emotional awareness with productivity demands. However, by recognizing these challenges and approaching them with empathy and understanding, teams can navigate them and unleash the potential for more meaningful connections, improved teamwork, and enduring achievements.

Emotional Intelligence in Decision Making

In the intricate dance of teamwork, where the rhythm is set by the collective beat of individual insights and shared aspirations, the sway of emotions in the decision-making process often goes unnoticed. Yet, these undercurrents of feeling, ranging from the subtle tug of intuition to the stormy seas of stress, play a pivotal role, influencing not only the paths chosen but the harmony of the journey itself. Recognizing and harnessing these emotional forces within team settings is a nuanced art, requiring a blend of keen observation, empathetic understanding, and strategic foresight.

The sway of emotions in decision-making is not a mere backdrop to the logical analysis but a dynamic interplay that shapes outcomes in profound ways. Consider the surge of enthusiasm that can propel a team towards innovative solutions, or the shadow of anxiety that may cast doubt on a risky yet potentially rewarding direction. These emotions, when acknowledged and understood, offer invaluable insights, serving as compasses that guide teams through the complex terrain of choices and consequences. However, the challenge lies not in merely recognizing these emotional undercurrents but in skillfully integrating this awareness into the team's decision-making fabric. By identifying and harnessing these emotional forces within team settings, leaders and team members can feel empowered to make decisions that not only make logical sense but also resonate on an emotional level, fostering a sense of unity and shared purpose.

Integrating emotional intelligence into collective decision-making processes begins by cultivating an environment where emotions are not only accepted but also valued as critical inputs. This environment encourages team members to voice their feelings and intuitions about various options, viewing these contributions as essential pieces of the decision-making puzzle. Facilitated discussions, where team members explore the emotional pros and cons of different paths, foster a deeper understanding of the potential impact of decisions, not just on the outcome but on the team's morale and motivation. Such discussions also highlight the importance of aligning emotions with organizational values and goals, ensuring that decisions resonate on both logical and emotional levels.

Finding the right balance between logic and emotion in team decision-making is akin to walking a tightrope, where the key to success lies in leaning into both without losing equilibrium. Teams skilled in this balance employ a process of reflective deliberation, in which logical analysis of facts and data is complemented by consideration of the emotional weight of decisions. This reflective process often involves scenario-planning exercises that not only map potential outcomes but also explore the emotional landscape associated with each scenario. By anticipating the emotional reactions to different courses of action, teams can make informed decisions that are both rationally sound and emotionally intelligent.

The potency of emotional intelligence in decision-making is vividly illustrated through a myriad of case studies, each shedding light on how teams, guided by emotional insights, navigate their way to superior outcomes. One such case involves a product launch team at a technology firm, standing at a crossroads between a safe, incremental update and a radical redesign that promised to redefine the market. The initial inclination towards the safer option, driven by a logical assessment of risks and rewards, was challenged by a deeper exploration of the team's emotional landscape. A series of facilitated discussions revealed a shared passion for innovation and a willingness to embrace risk, underpinned by a strong belief in the company's vision. This emotional alignment tipped the scales in favor of the bold redesign, leading to a launch that not only exceeded market expectations but also galvanized the team around a renewed sense of purpose and pride.

Another case study from a non-profit organization tasked with reallocating resources under budget constraints showcases the role of empathy in decision-making. Faced with difficult choices that would affect both the scope of their programs and the morale of their staff, the leadership team adopted an emotionally intelligent approach. Through empathetic engagement with stakeholders and reflective consideration of the emotional dimensions of various options, the team devised a solution that balanced financial sustainability with a minimal impact on staff and beneficiaries. This decision, rooted in both rational analysis and emotional understanding, not only preserved the organization's integrity but also reinforced the team's cohesion and commitment to their mission.

These instances, among countless others, underscore the transformative power of integrating emotional intelligence into team decision-making. In recognizing and valuing the emotional undercurrents that influence choices, teams not only enhance their capacity for innovative and empathetic solutions but also strengthen the bonds that unite them. This integration of emotional insights with logical analysis becomes not just a strategy for effective decision-making but a catalyst for building teams that are resilient, motivated, and deeply connected to their shared goals and to each other.

Nurturing a Culture of Feedback and Growth

Within the intricate landscape of team interactions, feedback stands out as a crucial element. It intricately intertwines with both personal and professional growth, possessing the power to either fortify or dismantle the team's unity. Far from a mere mechanism of critique, feedback, when cultivated within a culture of growth, transforms into a powerful catalyst for evolution and innovation. It is within this nuanced interplay of exchange that team members find space to stretch their capabilities, refine their talents, and step into the broader expanse of their potential. Yet, the journey to embed feedback as a natural and welcome aspect of team life requires more than intention; it demands a deliberate reimagining of input as a communal endeavor, supported by an environment that champions safety, trust, and the mutual pursuit of excellence.

Feedback as a Growth Tool

The alchemy of transforming feedback from a source of apprehension into a tool for growth lies in recognizing its dual capacity to illuminate strengths and reveal areas for improvement gently. This dual capacity, when harnessed within teams, fosters an atmosphere where learning and development are not just encouraged but are celebrated as integral to the team's journey. Feedback, in this light, becomes a beacon, guiding each member not only to achieve their best but also to elevate the team's collective performance. It shifts the paradigm from feedback as a critique to feedback as a gift offered and received with the intent of mutual growth and understanding.

Creating Safe Spaces for Feedback

The cornerstone of a feedback-rich culture is cultivating spaces perceived as safe, where vulnerability is not a liability but a sign of trust and commitment to growth. Achieving this perception begins with leadership that models openness to feedback, demonstrating a willingness to listen, reflect, and, most importantly, act on the insights gained. This modeling sets a precedent, signaling to team members that feedback is not only safe but is a valued aspect of team engagement. Further, the establishment of clear guidelines around feedback, its purpose, its delivery, and its reception, lays the groundwork for interactions that are respectful, constructive, and oriented towards growth. These guidelines act as the boundaries within which feedback exchanges occur, ensuring that even when the truths shared are complex, they are enveloped in a spirit of care and respect.

The Role of Emotional Intelligence in Feedback

At the heart of effective feedback exchanges lies emotional intelligence, the unseen yet palpable force that informs both the delivery and reception of feedback. Emotional intelligence, with its roots in empathy, self-awareness, and social awareness, guides team members to approach feedback not as an ego exercise but as an act of engagement. It encourages the giver of feedback to tailor their message, considering not only the words but also the timing, setting, and emotional state of the recipient. This tailored approach ensures that feedback is not just heard but is truly listened to, processed, and integrated. Simultaneously, emotional intelligence equips the receiver of feedback with the resilience to listen openly, to sift through the discomfort of critique, and to find the valuable nuggets of truth that spur growth. This dual application of emotional intelligence turns feedback sessions into rich dialogues, where insights flow freely, and growth is ignited.

Implementing a Feedback Culture

Strategic steps mark the path to embedding a culture of feedback within a team, each designed to build upon the last, gradually weaving input into the very fabric of team interaction. Initiating regular feedback sessions, scheduled to the rhythm of the team's workflow, ensures that feedback becomes a consistent part of team life, not relegated to annual reviews or sporadic moments of crisis. These sessions, whether structured as one-on-ones or as team roundtables, provide regular checkpoints for reflection, assessment, and planning.

In parallel, the introduction of tools and platforms that facilitate feedback exchange, whether digital platforms that allow for anonymous feedback or structured templates for sharing insights, removes barriers to participation. These tools offer diverse avenues for feedback, accommodating team members' varying comfort levels and preferences.

Moreover, the celebration of feedback successes, instances where feedback has led to noticeable improvements or achievements, reinforces the value of the feedback process. Highlighting these successes, whether in team meetings or through internal communications, serves as a vivid reminder of the tangible benefits of feedback, bolstering the team's commitment to this culture of growth.

In nurturing this culture, where feedback is woven into the team's daily interactions and processes, leaders and members together cultivate a garden of growth. This garden, tended with care, respect, and a shared dedication to excellence, flourishes, producing not only outstanding results but a team deeply connected by the mutual pursuit of their best selves.

The Emotional Intelligence of Negotiation

In the intricate weave of team dynamics, the fabric of negotiation holds a particularly vibrant thread, its colors deepened by the rich hues of emotional intelligence (EI). Here, within the nuanced interplay of differing perspectives and competing interests, lies an arena where the mastery of emotions becomes not merely advantageous but quintessential, for it is through the prism of EI that negotiation transforms from a battleground of contention into a dance of concord, where each step is measured not only by strategic intent but by a keen sensitivity to the emotional undercurrents that sway the rhythm of dialogue.

Negotiation Skills and EI

The essence of negotiation, often misconceived as a mere exchange of wants, transcends the transactional to touch the very core of human interaction. At this juncture, emotional intelligence emerges as the compass that guides negotiators away from the shoals of misunderstanding toward the haven of mutual satisfaction. It equips them with the foresight to anticipate reactions, the empathy to understand opposing viewpoints, and the self-regulation to maintain composure under pressure. This trinity of emotional competencies imbues negotiators with an aura of authenticity, fostering an atmosphere where openness prevails over obfuscation and trust gradually eclipses trepidation.

Understanding Needs and Emotions

Central to the art of negotiation is the recognition that beneath the veneer of demands lie deeper needs and emotions, often unspoken yet profoundly influential. To navigate this terrain with finesse requires attunement to the subtle cues that betray inner states: a pause too prolonged, a gaze averted, a tone tinged with frustration. By attuning to these signals, an emotionally intelligent negotiator discerns not just the what of the negotiation but the why, peeling back layers to reveal the underlying needs that fuel the discourse. In this revelation lies the key to crafting proposals that resonate on a deeper emotional level, transforming negotiation from a zero-sum game to a symphony of aligned interests.

Strategies for Emotionally Intelligent Negotiation

The deployment of emotionally intelligent strategies within negotiation contexts demands not only an acute awareness of one's emotional landscape but also a deliberate intention to foster positive emotional states in all parties involved. One such strategy is cultivating positive rapport from the outset, setting a tone of camaraderie that serves as a buffer against the inevitable tensions that negotiations may create. This rapport, built on small gestures of genuine interest and respect, lays the groundwork for a collaborative rather than adversarial engagement.

Another pivotal strategy is reflective listening, in which the negotiator echoes the counterpart's sentiments and concerns, validating their emotions and demonstrating understanding. This practice not only deepens empathy but also clarifies misunderstandings, ensuring that responses are tailored to address the heart of the issue rather than its superficial trappings.

Moreover, the strategic disclosure of vulnerabilities or concessions, when timed with precision, can disarm and humanize, bridging gaps of distrust. Such disclosures, however, must be wielded with discernment, balanced carefully to avoid exploitation while signaling a commitment to equitable outcomes.

Training for EI in Negotiation

The cultivation of emotional intelligence in negotiation transcends the individual, requiring a systemic approach to training that embeds EI principles into the very fabric of team development. Workshops that simulate negotiation scenarios, coupled with real-time feedback on emotional responses, offer a dynamic platform for honing these skills. These simulations, designed to mirror the complexities of real-world negotiations, challenge participants to navigate emotional undercurrents, practice empathetic listening, and self-regulate in the heat of discourse.

In addition, integrating mindfulness practices into training regimens enhances emotional awareness, equipping team members with the clarity to discern their emotional states and the agility to adapt their strategies accordingly. Mindfulness, with its emphasis on present-moment awareness, serves as a bulwark against reactive impulses that can derail negotiations, fostering instead a responsiveness grounded in a calm, measured assessment.

Peer coaching circles further enrich this training landscape, providing a space for ongoing reflection and growth. Within these circles, team members share experiences, dissecting both successes and setbacks to distill insights that refine their negotiation prowess. This collective inquiry not only accelerates learning but also reinforces the ethos of emotional intelligence as a shared journey, one that elevates not just the individual but the entire team.

In the orchestration of negotiation, where outcomes hinge on the delicate balance between assertiveness and empathy, between persuasion and understanding, emotional intelligence shines as the guiding star. It informs every gesture, every word, every silence, imbuing negotiators with the depth of insight and the breadth of compassion needed to navigate the complex human dimensions of negotiation. With each emotionally intelligent exchange, the possibility of win-win outcomes becomes not just an aspiration but a tangible reality, a testament to the transformative power of emotional intelligence in the art and science of negotiation.

Celebrating Diversity: Emotional Intelligence and Inclusion

Within the complex interplay of team dynamics, emotional intelligence (EI) is a powerful yet often understated force. It knits together a fabric of inclusivity and respect, fostering a cohesive, harmonious environment. This nuanced understanding and management of emotions serve not only as a bridge across the chasms of cultural and personal differences but also as a catalyst for transforming these differences into a vibrant source of innovation and strength. In the realm of diversity, where the richness of varied perspectives and experiences offers untold potential for growth, the application of emotional intelligence becomes a critical endeavor, enabling teams to transcend mere tolerance to embrace a deep appreciation of each unique thread in the organizational fabric.

At its essence, the role of emotional intelligence in fostering an inclusive environment pivots on its ability to cultivate empathy, a profound understanding that stretches beyond the confines of one's own experience to appreciate the diverse realities of others. This empathy, grounded in emotional awareness and regulation, enables team members and leaders alike to navigate the nuanced expressions of identity and culture with sensitivity and grace. It is through this empathetic lens that diversity is not just acknowledged but celebrated, recognized not as a box to be ticked but as a wellspring of creativity, insight, and resilience.

The journey towards an inclusive team environment, enriched by diversity and guided by emotional intelligence, begins with a deliberate effort to understand and value the multifaceted nature of human identity. This effort extends beyond acknowledging visible differences to a deeper engagement with the varied life experiences, cultural backgrounds, and personal stories that shape each team member's perspective. Interactive workshops that explore themes of identity, privilege, and bias offer fertile ground for this engagement, providing safe spaces for reflection, dialogue, and the sharing of experiences. These sessions, facilitated with an emphasis on emotional intelligence, encourage participants to confront their assumptions, to listen with an open heart, and to forge connections that span the divides of background and belief.

Leadership, in this context, plays a pivotal role, embodying principles of inclusivity through practices that celebrate diversity and foster a sense of belonging for all team members. Inclusive leaders harness their emotional intelligence to create environments where every voice is heard and valued, where differences are not merely tolerated but are actively sought and leveraged. They demonstrate this commitment through transparent communication practices that reflect awareness of and sensitivity to their team's diverse needs and preferences. Regular check-ins, tailored to accommodate diverse communication and interaction styles, exemplify this approach, ensuring that each team member feels seen, heard, and understood.

Moreover, inclusive leaders employ decision-making processes that are participatory and democratic, valuing diverse team member inputs and recognizing the unique insights each perspective brings. This approach not only enhances the quality and creativity of decisions but also reinforces the principles of equity and respect that lie at the heart of an inclusive team culture.

The transformative impact of leveraging emotional intelligence to embrace and celebrate diversity is vividly illustrated in the success stories of teams across industries and sectors. One such narrative unfolds within a global technology firm, where a concerted effort to understand and value cultural differences led to the development of a product that resonated across multiple markets, driving unprecedented growth. This success was rooted in the team's ability to draw on its members' diverse cultural insights, guided by a leadership that recognized and valued this richness.

Another story emerges from a healthcare nonprofit, where the diversity of the team, spanning a wide range of ages, backgrounds, and experiences, initially posed challenges to communication and collaboration. Through workshops focused on building emotional intelligence, particularly in the areas of empathy and inclusive communication, the team developed a deeper understanding and appreciation of each other's perspectives. This newfound unity and respect translated into innovative approaches to service delivery, significantly enhancing the organization's impact on underserved communities.

These stories, and many others, underscore the power of emotional intelligence as a tool for fostering inclusivity and leveraging diversity. They highlight the journey from acknowledging differences to valuing and celebrating them, a journey that is both challenging and deeply rewarding. Through this process, teams not only enhance their capacity for innovation and performance but also contribute to building a more inclusive, empathetic, and just world.

As we conclude this exploration of emotional intelligence's role in celebrating diversity and fostering inclusion within teams, we are reminded of the profound impact that empathy, understanding, and respect can have on the fabric of organizational life. This journey, marked by a commitment to valuing every individual's unique contributions and creating environments where all can thrive, is not just a pathway to enhanced team performance but a testament to the transformative power of emotional intelligence in shaping a more inclusive and vibrant future.

Chapter Summary:
Enhancing Team Dynamics

Creating Cohesive Teams: The Role of Emotional Awareness

- Emotional awareness is essential for building strong team cohesion. Leaders who are attuned to their team's emotional landscape can transform potential conflicts into opportunities for bonding. By recognizing emotions and fostering an empathetic environment, leaders lay the groundwork for a supportive, connected team.

Building Emotional Bonds

- Strategies like team retreats and shared activities encourage open communication and help team members connect on a personal level. Activities that reveal individual values and aspirations foster understanding and appreciation, both vital for building a strong emotional foundation within the team.

Emotional Awareness Exercises

- Exercises such as active listening, the 'emotion wheel,' and role reversals deepen emotional connections within teams. These activities promote empathy, encourage openness about emotions, and enhance overall team cohesion, thereby improving collaboration and decision-making.

Success Stories

- Teams that prioritize emotional awareness report improved dynamics, morale, and performance. For instance, a development team facing delays used emotional awareness techniques to reduce tension and improve efficiency. Similarly, a marketing team struggling with internal competition embraced empathy-building exercises to foster a collaborative culture, boosting creativity and cohesion.

Emotional Intelligence in Decision-Making

- Emotions significantly influence decision-making. Teams that incorporate emotional intelligence into their decision-making processes can align choices with both logical analysis and emotional resonance, creating a balanced approach that fosters unity and shared purpose.

Balancing Logic and Emotion

- Teams skilled in emotional intelligence integrate emotional and logical perspectives through reflective deliberation. By acknowledging emotional implications alongside factual considerations, they make well-rounded decisions that align with team values and organizational goals.

Decision-Making Case Studies

- Examples illustrate how emotionally intelligent decision-making leads to superior outcomes. For instance, a tech team chose a bold product redesign after recognizing the team's shared passion for innovation. Similarly, a non-profit balanced financial challenges with empathetic decision-making, preserving morale and commitment.

Nurturing a Culture of Feedback and Growth

- Feedback, when framed as a tool for growth, helps team members stretch their capabilities and develop skills. A culture of feedback requires safe spaces where vulnerability is respected, and emotional intelligence guides the delivery and reception of feedback.

Creating Safe Spaces for Feedback

- Leaders who model openness and respect foster a culture of feedback. Guidelines for constructive feedback ensure that exchanges are purposeful, respectful, and aimed at mutual improvement. Emotional intelligence underpins these interactions, helping team members approach feedback as a path to personal and collective growth.

Implementing a Feedback Culture

- Regular feedback sessions, tools for anonymous input, and celebrating successes all reinforce the importance of feedback. This approach creates an environment where continuous learning and improvement are woven into the team's daily routines.

The Emotional Intelligence of Negotiation

- Emotional intelligence transforms negotiation from a transactional exchange to a collaborative process. Leaders skilled in EI can recognize underlying emotions, establish rapport, and create win-win outcomes by balancing assertiveness with empathy.

Negotiation Skills and EI

- Emotionally intelligent negotiators anticipate reactions, understand perspectives, and maintain composure under pressure. By building rapport and practicing reflective listening, they foster a cooperative atmosphere that leads to mutually beneficial results.

Strategies for Emotionally Intelligent Negotiation

- Key strategies include building rapport, using reflective listening, and strategically disclosing vulnerabilities to build trust. These approaches create a negotiation environment focused on understanding and shared goals rather than competition.

Celebrating Diversity: Emotional Intelligence and Inclusion

- Emotional intelligence fosters inclusivity by encouraging empathy and understanding of diverse perspectives. This inclusivity transforms diversity from a checkbox to a wellspring of creativity as team members leverage their unique backgrounds to enhance collaboration and innovation.

Leadership's Role in Inclusivity

- Inclusive leaders use emotional intelligence to build environments where all voices are heard and respected. By modeling inclusivity and promoting open communication, they create a culture of belonging that values each team member's contributions.

Diversity Success Stories

- Stories from various industries showcase how emotional intelligence and inclusivity drive success. For example, a tech firm utilized cultural insights to launch a globally successful product, and a healthcare nonprofit used empathy training to strengthen team unity and enhance service delivery.

Conclusion

This chapter underscores the transformative role of emotional intelligence in team dynamics. By fostering emotional awareness, integrating emotions into decision-making, nurturing a culture of feedback, and celebrating diversity, teams not only improve performance but also build a foundation of mutual respect and understanding. These practices create teams that are resilient, innovative, and deeply connected.

NINE

PERSONAL AND PROFESSIONAL GROWTH THROUGH EMOTIONAL INTELLIGENCE

A blank canvas holds infinite possibilities, just as the dawn of each new day offers an opportunity to paint our lives with the vibrant colors of growth and learning. Emotional intelligence (EI) acts as the palette from which we draw not only the hues of self-awareness and empathy but also the shades of resilience and adaptability that define our personal and professional landscapes. In this journey, setting emotional goals is comparable to laying the initial brushstroke on our life's canvas. It's a purposeful decision that influences the direction of our growth and enhances the quality of our interactions.

Setting Emotional Goals: A Path to Growth

Unlike traditional objectives that often focus on external accomplishments, emotional goals emphasize internal growth, aiming to enhance our emotional landscape. This 'emotional landscape' refers to the overall quality and richness of our emotional experiences, including our ability to understand and manage our own emotions, as well as our capacity for empathy and effective social interaction. It's a journey of empowerment, much like a gardener who knows that the beauty of the rose lies not just in its bloom but in the strength of its roots and the health of the soil it grows from.

To embark on this path, begin by reflecting on moments when emotions have led you astray or when a lack of understanding has clouded your judgment. Perhaps it was a heated discussion where anger got the best of you, or a time when anxiety clouded your decision-making abilities. These instances serve as signposts, guiding you towards areas ripe for growth.

Identifying Emotional Growth Areas

Pinpointing the specific aspects of emotional intelligence that warrant attention is the next step. This requires a candid self-assessment, where honesty paves the way for meaningful progress. Tools such as the Emotional Competence Inventory (ECI) offer a structured approach to this self-evaluation, providing insights into the various dimensions of EI, including self-awareness, self-regulation, social skills, empathy, and motivation.

For a practical exercise, consider maintaining an emotional diary for a week. This diary is a tool for self-reflection, where you can document instances where emotions have significantly influenced your behavior or decisions. At the end of the week, review your entries to identify patterns or recurring themes. This exercise not only sharpens your self-awareness but also highlights specific areas for improvement, setting the stage for targeted emotional growth.

Creating a Personal Growth Plan

With a clear understanding of your emotional growth areas, the next step is to craft a personal growth plan that outlines actionable steps towards achieving your emotional goals. These goals should be specific, measurable, achievable, relevant, and time-bound (SMART). For instance, a particular goal could be to improve your self-awareness by recognizing and labeling your emotions in the moment. A measurable step could be to do this at least three times a day. This plan ensures that each goal is grounded in reality and accompanied by a clear roadmap for achieving it.

For instance, if one of your goals is to enhance your empathy, a measurable step could be to engage in active listening during conversations, dedicating at least one interaction each day to fully focus on understanding the other person's perspective without judgment or interruption. Document these interactions in your emotional diary, noting any challenges faced and progress made.

Tracking and Reflecting on Progress

The journey towards emotional intelligence is continuous, with each step forward offering new insights and opportunities for growth. It's a journey that requires your full engagement and commitment. Regularly tracking your progress is essential, providing tangible evidence of your development and helping maintain momentum. Use your emotional diary as a tool for this reflection, comparing your current emotional responses and interactions with those documented at the beginning of your journey.

At predetermined intervals, perhaps monthly or quarterly, set aside time for a comprehensive review of your progress. Reflect on the goals you've achieved, the challenges you've encountered, and the lessons learned along the way. This reflection not only celebrates your growth but also informs future goals, ensuring that your journey towards emotional intelligence remains dynamic and responsive to your evolving needs.

In addition, consider sharing your experiences with a trusted mentor or peer. This exchange offers an external perspective on your progress, providing encouragement, accountability, and valuable insights that can further enrich your journey.

The pursuit of emotional intelligence, marked by the setting and achievement of emotional goals, offers a pathway to profound personal and professional transformation. This journey, grounded in self-awareness, guided by empathy, and enriched by continuous learning, not only enhances our interactions and relationships but also empowers us to navigate the complexities of life with grace and resilience. As we dedicate ourselves to this endeavor, we find that the canvas of our lives, once blank, becomes a masterpiece of growth, learning, and emotional depth.

Setting SMART Emotional Goals

The process of setting emotional goals follows the same principles as achieving other personal and professional objectives: the SMART framework. SMART goals encourage focus, clarity, and motivation, making the process of developing emotional intelligence more effective and trackable. Below, we'll break down each element of the SMART framework as it applies to emotional goals, followed by specific examples to bring these ideas to life.

- **Specific** - An emotional goal needs to be precise and clearly defined. Instead of aiming to "be less reactive," for example, you could set a goal to "practice deep breathing techniques whenever I feel frustrated during a conversation." A specific goal identifies a clear behavior and situational context, making it easier to understand and work towards.
  - **Example**: "I want to improve my empathy by actively listening without interrupting when my partner talks about their day."
- **Measurable** - Having measurable goals is essential for tracking progress and recognizing achievements. Emotional goals may feel intangible, but adding a quantitative element helps gauge development over time. This could be the frequency with which you perform a behavior or a scale to rate your responses.
  - **Example**: "I will practice active listening at least three times a week and use a journal to record my reflections afterward, rating my effort on a scale from 1 to 5."

- **Achievable** - An achievable goal is realistic and within your ability to complete, given your resources and constraints. Setting manageable goals prevents discouragement and helps maintain momentum. For instance, aiming to eliminate all anger responses might be too ambitious initially, but reducing their intensity can be more feasible.
  - **Example**: "When I feel irritated at work, I will take a five-minute walk to cool down before responding, practicing this at least twice a week."
- **Relevant** - Your goals should be aligned with your personal growth and values. Setting emotional goals that are meaningful to your specific life circumstances increases commitment. Identify the areas of emotional intelligence you want to develop, and ensure your goals directly contribute to them.
  - **Example**: "To improve my relationships, I want to become more empathetic by learning about my friends' hobbies and interests. I will ask questions and actively listen during our conversations."
- **Time-Bound** - A time-bound goal includes a clear deadline, which adds a sense of urgency and helps avoid procrastination. For example, you might aim to reduce your stress response by a certain percentage within three months, giving yourself a deadline to measure against.
  - **Example**: "Within the next month, I will reduce my emotional outbursts by 50% by using relaxation techniques and self-talk. I will track these occurrences weekly to evaluate progress."

Examples of SMART Emotional Goals

To make this framework even more actionable, here are some examples of SMART, emotional goals, complete with timelines and measurement strategies:

- **Goal**: "Over the next 30 days, I will improve my self-regulation by practicing a grounding technique each time I experience stress at work."
  - *Specific*: Practicing a grounding technique (such as counting breaths or naming objects in the room).
  - *Measurable*: Aim to use the technique at least once per day during stressful situations.
  - *Achievable*: This requires only a few minutes and can be done discreetly.
  - *Relevant*: Addresses self-regulation, a key aspect of emotional intelligence.
  - *Time-Bound*: Daily for the next 30 days.

- **Goal**: "I will deepen my empathy within the next two months by reading one book each month about a culture different from my own and discussing what I learned with a friend or colleague."
  - *Specific*: Reading one book on cultural topics and discussing it with others.
  - *Measurable*: Two books over two months with follow-up conversations.
  - *Achievable*: Reading one book a month is realistic for most schedules.
  - *Relevant*: Expands empathy and cultural understanding.
  - *Time-Bound*: Completion in two months.

Tracking Progress on Emotional Goals

Tracking progress is essential to staying on course and understanding the effectiveness of your efforts. Here are some methods for monitoring your emotional growth:

- **Journaling**: Dedicate a notebook or digital document to reflecting on your experiences with your goals. Write down any triggers, reactions, and outcomes, as well as how you felt before and after practicing emotional regulation techniques. Regularly noting these reflections will provide insights into your growth over time.

- **Self-Rating Scales**: Use a simple scale from 1 to 10 to rate your responses to situations. For instance, if your goal is to reduce frustration, rate the intensity of your frustration each time you encounter a trigger. Over time, you should see the ratings decrease.
- **Weekly Check-ins**: Set aside time each week to evaluate how well you met your goals. Reflect on your progress and adjust your strategies if needed. If you're working on empathy, for example, consider how often you actively listened without interrupting or how many new perspectives you've engaged with.
- **Accountability Partner**: Partnering with a friend or colleague can help maintain motivation. Share your goals and updates with them, and ask them to provide feedback or check in with you regularly. Knowing that someone else is aware of your goals can create gentle pressure to stay on track.

By setting SMART emotional goals and tracking your progress, you're taking tangible steps toward enhancing your emotional intelligence. This focused, structured approach empowers you to make incremental improvements that, over time, lead to lasting changes in how you understand, regulate, and express emotions in various aspects of your life.

The Role of Emotional Intelligence in Career Advancement

In the vast expanse of the professional world, where ambition intertwines with capability, emotional intelligence (EI) emerges as a beacon, guiding individuals through the complexities of workplace dynamics towards the pinnacle of career success. This nuanced amalgam of self-awareness, empathy, and adept social navigation proves not merely advantageous but pivotal, redefining pathways to advancement and reconfiguring the essence of leadership. Empathy, in particular, forms the heart of emotional intelligence, fostering connections and understanding in the professional realm. It helps us understand others' perspectives and feelings, thereby improving our communication, collaboration, and leadership skills.

EI and Career Success

The terrain of modern careers, characterized by rapid evolution and the blurring of traditional hierarchies, demands more than technical expertise and a commendable work ethic. It calls for an astute understanding of the emotional currents that sway decision-making, team cohesion, and leadership effectiveness. Emotional intelligence, with its capacity to decipher these undercurrents, becomes the linchpin of career progression. It transforms challenges into stepping stones and interactions into opportunities, ensuring that one's professional journey is not just a climb but a meaningful ascent marked by profound connections and impactful achievements.

In this context, the ability to manage one's emotions and to read and respond to others' emotions becomes a differentiator, setting apart leaders who inspire and motivate from those who merely direct. It's the emotionally intelligent leader who navigates crises with composure, fosters a culture of trust and respect, and, by virtue of these abilities, ascends in their career, leaving a trail of influence and inspiration.

Developing EI for Career Growth

The cultivation of emotional intelligence as a strategy for career growth involves a meticulous process of introspection, learning, and practice. It begins with a commitment to self-discovery, to peeling back the layers of one's emotional reactions, triggers, and tendencies. Tools such as 360-degree feedback, which provide feedback from peers, subordinates, and supervisors, and emotional intelligence assessments offer valuable insights into one's EI landscape, highlighting strengths to leverage and gaps to bridge.

The transition from insight to action involves deliberate practice: a conscious effort to employ strategies that enhance emotional regulation, empathy, and social skills. For instance, a professional aiming to improve their empathetic listening might practice focusing entirely on understanding colleagues' perspectives during conversations, resisting the urge to interrupt or to formulate responses prematurely. Similarly, developing the ability to manage stress and maintain emotional equilibrium in high-pressure situations might involve techniques such as mindfulness meditation or cognitive restructuring to challenge and change distressing thought patterns.

Networking and Relationships

The complex process of networking, often seen as merely a transactional exchange of contacts and opportunities, transforms under the influence of emotional intelligence into a vibrant mosaic of meaningful relationships. Here, the ability to forge genuine relationships based on mutual respect and understanding becomes a cornerstone of professional networking. Emotionally intelligent networking transcends the superficial, embracing a deeper engagement with peers, mentors, and industry leaders. It's about listening with intent, sharing with sincerity, and offering support without the immediate expectation of return. This approach not only enriches one's professional network but also embeds one in a supportive, enriching community of practice, facilitating career advancement through shared knowledge, opportunities, and advocacy.

In practice, emotionally intelligent networking involves reaching out to others with a genuine interest in their work and well-being, celebrating their successes, and offering assistance in times of need. It's about consistently contributing to professional communities, whether through knowledge sharing, mentorship, or collaboration, thereby cultivating a reputation as a valuable and supportive member of one's professional ecosystem.

Case Studies

The narratives of individuals who have harnessed emotional intelligence to ascend in their careers illuminate the tangible impact of EI on professional advancement. One such story is that of a mid-level manager in a multinational corporation whose adeptness at managing team dynamics and resolving conflicts, with empathy and insight, caught the attention of senior leadership. Her ability to navigate complex emotional landscapes, ensuring team cohesion and high performance even in challenging times, led to her promotion to a leadership role in a high-stakes project. Her success in this capacity, marked by significant contributions to the project and the cultivation of a highly motivated, cohesive team, further propelled her career, establishing her as a key leader within the organization.

Another case involves an entrepreneur who, recognizing the value of emotional intelligence in building business relationships, prioritized EI development in his growth strategy. By focusing on understanding and addressing clients' and partners' emotional needs and motivations, he built strong, lasting relationships that sustained his business's growth. His reputation for integrity, empathy, and emotional savvy attracted top talent and loyal clients, driving the success of his venture and establishing him as a respected figure in his industry.

These stories, among countless others, underscore the transformative power of emotional intelligence in career advancement. They highlight how the mastery of EI not only facilitates professional growth but also enriches the journey with meaningful relationships, impactful leadership, and a profound sense of fulfillment. In the ever-evolving landscape of professional development, emotional intelligence stands as a steadfast ally, guiding individuals not only to the heights of career success but also to the depths of personal growth and connection.

Overcoming Imposter Syndrome
with Emotional Intelligence

Understanding Imposter Syndrome

Within the intricacies of personal and professional development lies a shadow that often dims the light of our accomplishments: imposter syndrome. This phenomenon, characterized by persistent self-doubt and fear of being exposed as a "fraud" despite evident success, weaves a complicated web of insecurity that entraps individuals in a cycle of anxiety and diminished self-worth. Unlike mere moments of uncertainty, imposter syndrome embeds itself in the psyche, whispering tales of inadequacy that contradict reality, leading to avoidance of further achievement or recognition out of fear of eventual unmasking. This paradoxical fear not only stifles growth but also erodes the joy and satisfaction derived from one's accomplishments, casting a long shadow over both personal satisfaction and professional progression.

The Role of Emotional Intelligence (EI) in Overcoming Imposter Syndrome

The battle against imposter syndrome unfolds on a profoundly emotional terrain, making emotional intelligence (EI) a critical ally. At the heart of EI lies the ability to navigate one's emotional landscape with understanding, acceptance, and strategy, turning the tide against the insidious whispers of imposter syndrome. The first step in this strategic navigation involves **self-awareness**, the cornerstone of EI, which illuminates the patterns of negative self-talk and irrational beliefs fueling imposter feelings. By holding a mirror to these distorted reflections of self, individuals gain the clarity needed to challenge and reframe them, replacing self-doubt with a grounded recognition of their abilities and worth.

Self-regulation, another pillar of EI, offers tools for managing the anxiety and emotional turmoil associated with imposter syndrome. Techniques such as mindfulness and cognitive-behavioral strategies empower individuals to calm the storm of impostorism, enabling a more rational evaluation of their fears and achievements. Through this emotional regulation, the grip of imposter syndrome loosens, giving way to a balanced perspective that acknowledges both strengths and areas for growth without descending into unfounded self-criticism.

Empathy, directed inward, transforms the harsh judgment often found in imposter syndrome into compassionate self-acceptance. Recognizing that perfection is an unattainable and unnecessary goal, individuals learn to celebrate progress and effort, fostering a kinder, more supportive internal dialogue. This empathetic self-view encourages risk-taking and growth, challenging the safety of the imposter's shadow in favor of the light of authentic achievement.

Case Studies: Overcoming Imposter Syndrome with EI

Case Study 1: The Young Professional Anna, a recent graduate, landed her dream job at a prestigious marketing firm. Despite her impressive academic record and positive feedback from her team, she constantly felt like a fraud. She feared her colleagues would eventually realize she wasn't as competent as they thought. After discussing these feelings with a mentor, Anna began practicing **self-awareness** by journaling her thoughts. She recorded each moment of self-doubt, noting the specific situations that triggered these feelings. By reflecting on these instances, she recognized a recurring pattern: she felt most inadequate when comparing herself to more experienced colleagues.

With this insight, Anna applied **self-regulation** techniques to reframe her thoughts. Each time self-doubt surfaced, she consciously reminded herself that comparing her beginning to someone else's middle wasn't fair or productive. She practiced cognitive reappraisal, intentionally replacing negative self-talk with affirmations of her unique skills and strengths. This process empowered her to appreciate her progress, leading to a gradual yet significant reduction in her imposter feelings.

Case Study 2: The Seasoned Executive James, with over 20 years of experience, was promoted to a high-stakes leadership role at a multinational company. He feared he wasn't equipped to lead such a diverse team and worried about being exposed as inadequate. Drawing on **empathy** and recognizing his need for self-compassion, James began to acknowledge his accomplishments and the hard work that brought him to this role.

He also shared his challenges with a close colleague, who helped him see that his willingness to express vulnerability made him a more approachable leader. This insight led him to accept that he didn't need to have all the answers immediately. By practicing **self-regulation** and using mindfulness exercises to calm his nerves before essential meetings, James gradually developed a renewed confidence in his abilities.

Practical Exercises: Building EI to Combat Imposter Syndrome

Here are several exercises to enhance self-awareness, self-regulation, and empathy as they relate to overcoming imposter syndrome:

1. **Thought Journaling and Reflection**
   - **Goal**: To gain insight into recurring thought patterns that contribute to imposter syndrome.
   - **Instructions**: Spend a few minutes each day reflecting on instances of self-doubt. Write down the situations that triggered these feelings, the thoughts that arose, and the emotional responses you experienced. After a week, review your entries to identify common themes and triggers.
   - **Outcome**: Increased self-awareness of the thoughts that fuel imposter syndrome, enabling you to anticipate and address them proactively.
2. **Cognitive Reappraisal Practice**
   - **Goal**: To develop the skill of reframing negative thoughts and reducing emotional intensity.

- ○ **Instructions**: When you catch yourself thinking negatively, pause for a moment. Ask yourself how you would view the situation if a friend were experiencing it instead of you. What supportive advice would you offer? Reframe the negative thought using this advice.
- ○ **Example**: Replace "I'm not good enough for this job" with "I'm continually learning and growing, and every experience adds to my skill set."
- ○ **Outcome**: Enhanced self-regulation and a more balanced perspective on personal abilities.

3. **Self-Compassion Meditation**
   - ○ **Goal**: To cultivate empathy towards oneself and foster a kinder inner dialogue.
   - ○ **Instructions**: Find a quiet, comfortable space to sit. Close your eyes and take a few deep breaths. Visualize a time when you felt insecure or doubted your abilities. As you hold this memory, imagine speaking to yourself as you would a friend, offering words of encouragement and understanding. Remind yourself that everyone experiences self-doubt and that your feelings are valid.
   - ○ **Outcome**: Increased self-empathy, helping to shift from self-criticism to self-compassion.

4. **Visualization Exercise: Acknowledging Achievements**
   - ○ **Goal**: To reinforce positive self-perception and internalize past successes.
   - ○ **Instructions**: At the end of each week, sit down and visualize the accomplishments you've achieved over the past few days, no matter how small. Picture yourself celebrating these successes and feeling pride in your efforts. Write down three things you're proud of from the week, focusing on what these achievements mean for your personal growth.
   - ○ **Outcome**: A more positive self-concept that diminishes the impact of imposter syndrome over time.

Final Thoughts on Imposter Syndrome

The path to overcoming imposter syndrome is one of continual growth and self-discovery. By integrating emotional intelligence practices into daily life, individuals can confront and reframe the self-doubt that holds them back. Cultivating self-awareness, practicing self-regulation, and nurturing self-compassion create a strong foundation for personal and professional development. Remember, imposter syndrome may whisper tales of inadequacy, but through EI, we find the courage to respond with a resounding affirmation of our true worth and potential.

Strategies for Building Self-Confidence

In shifting from the shadows of imposter syndrome to the light of authentic self-assurance, emotional intelligence offers a suite of strategies to fortify self-confidence. Here are some specific practices to help develop and sustain a strong sense of self-assurance:

1. **Positive Affirmations: Rewiring Self-Perception** - Positive affirmations involve acknowledging and reinforcing your own strengths, accomplishments, and values. This practice directly counteracts the cycle of self-doubt by replacing negative thought patterns with positive, empowering beliefs. Here's how to integrate affirmations into your daily routine:
   - **Journaling**: Each morning or evening, take a few minutes to write down three affirmations about yourself. These could be qualities you admire, achievements you're proud of, or goals you are confidently pursuing. For example, you might write, "I am a capable and skilled professional who brings value to my team," or "I handle challenges with resilience and grace."
   - **Verbal Affirmations**: Stand in front of a mirror and speak your affirmations out loud. Hearing yourself vocalize these positive statements can have a powerful effect on your subconscious mind, helping to shift your self-perception

over time. Choose affirmations that feel authentic and specific to you, such as "I am deserving of the success I've worked for" or "I approach each task with confidence and clarity."

- o **Affirmation Reminders**: Set up reminders on your phone or post affirmations around your workspace. These small prompts can serve as reinforcements throughout the day, keeping you focused on your strengths and fostering a positive mindset.

2. **Practicing Self-Compassion: Cultivating a Kinder Inner Dialogue** - Self-compassion involves treating yourself with the same kindness and understanding that you would offer to a friend. Instead of allowing critical self-judgment to dominate, self-compassion fosters a supportive, nurturing inner dialogue. Here are some practical ways to develop this practice:

- o **Mindfulness Meditation**: Begin a meditation session by focusing on your breath and noticing any self-critical thoughts that arise. Instead of engaging with these thoughts, acknowledge them and let them pass. Try to cultivate a compassionate response, such as, "It's okay to feel this way," or "I'm learning and growing each day." This helps train your mind to respond more gently to self-doubt.

- o **Self-Compassion Journaling**: Write a letter to yourself as you would to a friend going through a challenging time. Acknowledge your feelings without judgment, validate your experience, and offer kind words of encouragement. For example, if you're feeling insecure after a work setback, you might write, "I know today was difficult, and it's okay to feel disappointed. Remember, setbacks are part of growth, and I have the resilience to move forward."

- o **Supportive Phrases**: During moments of self-doubt, have a set of supportive phrases ready to ground you. Phrases like "I am doing my best" or "I am worthy of patience and understanding" can serve as gentle reminders to treat yourself with empathy.

3. **Goal Setting and Celebrating Success: Creating a Foundation of Accomplishment** - Setting realistic and achievable goals that align with your aspirations provides a roadmap for growth and allows you to measure progress over time. Each small success reinforces a sense of competence and builds self-confidence. Here's how to approach goal setting with a focus on self-confidence:

   - **SMART Goals**: Break down larger aspirations into Specific, Measurable, Achievable, Relevant, and Time-bound (SMART) goals. For instance, instead of setting a vague goal like "become a better public speaker," you could set a SMART goal: "Practice public speaking for 15 minutes daily, to give a five-minute presentation by the end of the month." Breaking goals into manageable steps allows you to make consistent progress.

   - **Celebrate Small Wins**: Each time you achieve a goal, take time to acknowledge and celebrate the accomplishment. Recognize the effort you put in, and appreciate your progress. It could be as simple as treating yourself to something you enjoy, writing about the experience in your journal, or sharing your success with a supportive friend or mentor.

   - **Reflection and Adjustment**: At the end of each week or month, reflect on your progress. Ask yourself which strategies worked well and what adjustments you might need to make. This process of reflection helps reinforce self-confidence by highlighting your progress and providing direction for future growth.

4. **Building Supportive Relationships: Leveraging Social Feedback for Confidence** - Developing supportive relationships is essential to building self-confidence, as these connections can offer valuable encouragement and

perspective. Here's how to cultivate and leverage a network that uplifts and reinforces your self-assurance:

- **Seek Feedback from Trusted Sources**: Regularly seek constructive feedback from colleagues, mentors, or friends who are genuinely invested in your success. Their insights can help you gain perspective on your strengths and identify areas for growth. Remember, positive feedback is often easier to accept when it comes from people you trust and respect.
- **Engage in Active Listening**: When someone offers praise or validation, make an effort to listen and truly absorb what they're saying. Resist the urge to dismiss compliments or deflect them with self-deprecating comments. Accepting positive feedback is an integral part of internalizing self-confidence.
- **Surround Yourself with Positive Influences**: Spend time with people who encourage and inspire you. Supportive relationships can help counterbalance any negative self-perceptions and provide a safe space for growth. Share your goals and aspirations with these individuals, and celebrate each other's progress as you pursue personal growth together.

By incorporating these specific strategies into daily life, you'll develop a robust foundation of self-confidence grounded in positive self-affirmation, self-compassion, meaningful goals, and supportive relationships. These practices, reinforced by the principles of emotional intelligence, allow you to navigate challenges with resilience and assurance, fostering a lasting sense of self-worth and personal empowerment.

Success Stories

The transformative power of emotional intelligence in overcoming imposter syndrome shines brightly in the stories of those who have navigated this journey. One such narrative involves a young software engineer who, despite her rapid ascent and accolades, grappled with crippling self-doubt. Through EI development, particularly in self-awareness and self-regulation, she began to challenge her imposter narrative, replacing it with evidence of her competence and achievements. Her journey from impostorism to self-assurance was marked by increased engagement in leadership roles, a testament to her newfound confidence.

Another tale of triumph emerged from a seasoned educator who felt like an imposter in academia, fearing exposure at any moment. By embracing empathy, both for herself and her students, she transformed her inner critic into a supportive guide, allowing her passion and knowledge to shine through without the shadow of a doubt. Her story, from imposter to empowered educator, inspires a reevaluation of self-worth and potential in the face of unfounded fears.

These stories, each unique yet universally resonant, underscore the efficacy of emotional intelligence in confronting and overcoming imposter syndrome. Through the strategic application of EI, the chains of self-doubt and fear are broken, replaced by a foundation of self-assurance and authentic living that supports both personal fulfillment and professional achievement.

Work-Life Balance: Managing Stress and Burnout

In an era where the boundaries between personal endeavors and professional pursuits have blurred, the quest for equilibrium necessitates more than mere time management; it demands a nuanced understanding of one's emotional landscape. This balance, delicate and often elusive, serves as a bulwark against the onslaught of stress and burnout, those twin specters that haunt the corridors of modern work life. Emotional intelligence, with its profound insights into self-regulation and empathy, offers a beacon of hope, illuminating strategies that not only mitigate stress but also foster a sustainable harmony between the demands of work and the joys of personal life.

The significance of achieving a harmonious work-life balance transcends avoiding professional burnout; it encompasses preserving one's well-being, nurturing relationships, and cultivating a fulfilling life beyond occupational roles. This equilibrium challenges the constant drive for productivity, highlighting that in the intricate mosaic of life, work constitutes just one piece among many, each symbolizing various aspects of who we are. Recognizing this interconnectedness and understanding the emotional toll of neglecting any one aspect is the first step toward achieving balance. Emotional intelligence sharpens this recognition, offering insights that guide us in prioritizing tasks, setting realistic expectations, and recognizing the signs of impending imbalance.

Emotional intelligence offers a suite of strategies for managing stress that go beyond conventional stress-relief techniques to address the root emotional triggers. Central to these strategies is mindfulness, an approach that encourages present-moment awareness and acceptance. Mindfulness, cultivated through meditation or simple breathing exercises, serves as an anchor, grounding us amidst the tumult of deadlines and responsibilities. It enables an acute awareness of stress signals, be it the tightening of shoulders, the quickening of breath, or the racing of thoughts, allowing for timely intervention before these signals burgeon into overwhelming anxiety. Additionally, emotional intelligence advocates for emotional venting in a controlled, healthy manner, whether through journaling, art, or conversation, providing a release valve for pent-up emotions and preventing the internalization of stress.

The art of setting boundaries, a skill honed through emotional intelligence, is pivotal in maintaining work-life balance. These boundaries, both physical and emotional, delineate the sacred space between professional obligations and personal time, ensuring that neither encroaches unduly upon the other. Emotional intelligence informs the negotiation of these boundaries, empowering individuals to communicate their needs assertively yet empathetically. It requires a deep understanding of one's limits and the courage to uphold them, even in the face of external pressures. This might manifest in practices as simple as designating technology-free zones or times, creating physical workspaces separate from living areas, or setting clear expectations with colleagues and family members regarding availability.

Preventing burnout, the final fortress against the erosion of work-life balance, relies heavily on the pillars of emotional intelligence. Burnout, with its hallmark symptoms of exhaustion, cynicism, and feelings of inefficacy, often creeps in unnoticed, making the ability to recognize its early signs crucial. Emotional intelligence sharpens this ability, enabling individuals to discern subtle shifts in their emotional state, motivation levels, and job satisfaction. It encourages proactive measures, from seeking support and reevaluating priorities to embracing self-compassion and rekindling passion for one's work. Moreover, emotional intelligence fosters resilience, the capacity to bounce back from setbacks and challenges without succumbing to burnout. This resilience is nurtured through practices that reinforce a positive outlook, cultivate a supportive network, and encourage engagement in activities that replenish one's emotional and physical energy.

In navigating the path toward work-life balance, emotional intelligence acts not only as a guide but also as a gardener, tending to the growth of practices and habits that sustain this balance. It reminds us that in the pursuit of professional achievements, we must not lose sight of the very essence that makes those achievements worthwhile: our well-being, our relationships, and our passions. Through emotional intelligence, we learn to harmonize the myriad demands of modern life, creating a symphony that resonates with the richness of a balanced existence.

The Continuous Learning Mindset: Growing Your Emotional Intelligence

The cultivation of emotional intelligence (EI) is not a task with a definitive endpoint but rather a dynamic process that evolves with each interaction, reflection, and insight. This fluidity demands a commitment to lifelong learning, an approach that views the development of EI not as a series of achievements but as an ongoing journey. The essence of this journey lies in recognizing that emotional landscapes shift, relationships transform, and professional environments change, necessitating an adaptable, open-minded approach to personal development.

In the realm of continuous learning, the concept of a growth mindset plays a pivotal role, serving as the fertile ground from which the seeds of emotional intelligence can sprout and flourish. A growth mindset, characterized by the belief that abilities and intelligence can be developed through dedication and hard work, provides a foundation for pursuing emotional mastery. It challenges the static view of intelligence as an immutable trait, opening the door to endless possibilities for enhancement and refinement. This mindset encourages individuals to view challenges as opportunities, setbacks as learning moments, and feedback as a valuable resource, driving the continuous development of EI.

Strategies for nurturing this perpetual growth in emotional intelligence are as diverse as the individuals pursuing them, yet they share a common thread of intentionality and purpose. Diving into the vast reservoir of knowledge available through books, articles, and research on emotional intelligence provides a theoretical framework that informs practice, offering insights into the complexities of human emotions and interactions. Supplementing this theoretical knowledge with practical experience, such as workshops, seminars, and EI-focused training programs, enables the application of concepts in real-world scenarios, bridging the gap between understanding and action.

Moreover, the digital age has ushered in an era of unprecedented access to learning resources, from online courses and webinars to virtual reality simulations and interactive apps designed to enhance emotional intelligence. These tools offer a personalized learning experience, allowing individuals to explore various aspects of EI at their own pace and in their own space. Engaging in these resources not only expands one's knowledge but also sharpens skills through practice and repetition, essential components of the learning process.

Self-reflection, an intrinsic aspect of emotional intelligence, serves as both a strategy for and a benefit of continuous learning. Regularly setting aside time to reflect on emotional reactions, decisions, and interactions fosters a deeper understanding of one's emotional patterns and triggers. This introspection, often facilitated by journaling or mindfulness practices, reveals insights into strengths and opportunities for growth, guiding the ongoing development of EI. It encourages a proactive stance towards personal and professional challenges, transforming them into catalysts for emotional and intellectual expansion.

The impact of a continuous learning approach to emotional intelligence extends far beyond personal satisfaction and professional success. It enriches relationships, enhances empathy, and fosters a resilient and adaptable demeanor, qualities that resonate across all spheres of life. This perpetual cycle of learning, applying, reflecting, and growing not only elevates the individual but also fosters emotionally intelligent communities and organizations where understanding, collaboration, and innovation thrive.

In this dynamic landscape of continuous learning, the journey of emotional intelligence becomes a lifelong adventure marked by discovery, transformation, and connection. Each step forward, each insight gained, and each skill honed contribute to a richer, more nuanced understanding of oneself and the world. This dedication to unending growth not only molds our emotional realm but also impacts the essence of our relationships and the direction of our professional lives, creating a rich and meaningful mosaic of experiences.

As we close this exploration of the continuous learning mindset and its role in developing emotional intelligence, we are reminded of the boundless potential within each of us. This journey, with its challenges and triumphs, underscores the transformative power of emotional intelligence in navigating the complexities of life and work. It invites us to remain curious, open, and dedicated to the pursuit of growth, ensuring that our journey of emotional intelligence is not just a path we travel but a landscape we enrich with every step.

Chapter Summary: Personal and Professional Growth Through Emotional Intelligence

Setting Emotional Goals: A Path to Growth

- Emotional goals focus on internal growth, shaping how we experience and manage our emotions. This journey involves self-reflection, where moments of emotional struggle act as signposts for improvement. Using tools such as an emotional diary and structured assessments, we can identify areas for growth, including empathy and emotional regulation.

Identifying Emotional Growth Areas

- Through candid self-assessment and tools such as the Emotional Competence Inventory (ECI), we gain insights into our emotional strengths and areas for improvement. Keeping an emotional diary over a week helps identify patterns and recurring themes, highlighting where we can target our efforts for growth.

Creating a Personal Growth Plan

- With clear goals in mind, the next step is to create a SMART-based growth plan. This plan includes specific, measurable steps, such as practicing active listening or labeling emotions. Tracking progress over time, possibly with a mentor, allows for regular reflection and adjustment, enriching the path toward emotional growth.

The Role of Emotional Intelligence in Career Advancement

- Emotional intelligence (EI) is a key asset in career success, offering an edge in navigating workplace dynamics and leading with empathy. EI fosters strong professional relationships and supports resilience in the face of challenges, helping individuals connect deeply and progress meaningfully in their careers.

Developing EI for Career Growth

- Cultivating EI for career advancement involves reflection, practice, and deliberate action. By honing skills such as empathy, stress management, and self-regulation, professionals can improve interactions and lead more effectively. Techniques like 360-degree feedback provide valuable insights, while practical applications like mindfulness strengthen these emotional skills.

Networking and Relationships

- Emotionally intelligent networking emphasizes genuine, supportive connections over transactional exchanges. By listening intently, celebrating others' successes, and contributing to professional communities, individuals build networks that support career growth and foster meaningful relationships.

Case Studies

- Stories of emotionally intelligent leaders illustrate how EI drives professional success. For example, a manager's empathetic leadership earned her recognition and career advancement, while an entrepreneur used EI to build lasting client relationships, fueling business growth. These cases highlight EI's role in career progression and relationship-building.

Overcoming Imposter Syndrome with Emotional Intelligence

- Imposter syndrome, characterized by self-doubt and fear of exposure, hinders personal growth. EI aids in overcoming this by promoting self-awareness, emotional regulation, and self-compassion. Through techniques like mindfulness and self-affirmation, individuals can reframe negative self-talk, embrace their achievements, and build self-confidence.

Strategies for Building Self-Confidence

- Emotional intelligence strategies for combating imposter syndrome include regular self-affirmation, seeking feedback, and setting realistic goals. These approaches encourage self-compassion and positive self-reflection, helping individuals grow their confidence and shift from self-doubt to self-assurance.

Work-Life Balance: Managing Stress and Burnout

- Emotional intelligence plays a pivotal role in maintaining work-life balance, providing strategies to manage stress and prevent burnout. By practicing mindfulness, setting boundaries, and recognizing signs of imbalance, individuals create a sustainable balance between work and personal life, preserving well-being and relationships.

The Continuous Learning Mindset: Growing Your Emotional Intelligence

- Emotional intelligence is a lifelong journey requiring a growth mindset. By embracing continuous learning, individuals can expand their EI through resources like books, workshops, and digital tools. Self-reflection, mindful practice, and a commitment to growth ensure that EI development remains an ongoing pursuit.

Impact of Continuous Learning on Emotional Intelligence

- Engaging in a cycle of learning, application, and reflection not only enriches personal growth but also enhances relationships, resilience, and adaptability. A continuous learning mindset supports both individual fulfillment and the creation of emotionally intelligent communities where collaboration and empathy thrive.

Conclusion

This chapter emphasizes the importance of setting emotional goals, developing EI for career advancement, and committing to lifelong learning. Through emotional intelligence, individuals can overcome challenges, achieve balance, and foster meaningful relationships, enriching both their personal and professional lives.

TEN

EMOTIONAL INTELLIGENCE
BEYOND BOUNDARIES

In the labyrinth of life's challenges, crises stand as formidable walls, seemingly insurmountable and fraught with uncertainty. Yet, within these walls lie hidden doors, gateways opened not by brute force but by the nuanced key of emotional intelligence (EI). While crises disrupt the familiar, scattering pieces of reality in their wake, they also lay bare the core of our resilience, our capacity to adapt, and the strength of our connections. Here, in the heart of turmoil, emotional intelligence becomes our compass, empowering us to navigate through the chaos with a sense of capability, control, and unwavering resolve.

This chapter, **Emotional Intelligence in Crisis Management**, explains how EI principles-self-awareness, self-regulation, empathy, and social skills-can change how we handle crises. Applying these skills turns challenges into opportunities for leadership, team unity, and personal growth, inspiring hope even in tough times.

Crisis as Opportunity

Crises, by their nature, test our limits. They strip away the veneer of routine, exposing the raw edges of our capabilities and vulnerabilities. Yet, it's precisely in these moments of vulnerability that the true potential for growth and leadership emerges. Emotional intelligence invites us to view crises through a different lens, seeing them not as insurmountable obstacles but as opportunities to apply our emotional skills in real-time, to lead with empathy, and to strengthen our connections with others.

Imagine a sudden market shift threatening a company's stability. Instead of panicking or blaming, an EI-aware leader recognizes their own emotions, stays calm, and assesses the situation clearly. They empathize with their team, validate fears, and guide everyone toward problem-solving. This transforms the crisis into a leadership opportunity, strengthening team resilience and adaptability.

Staying Grounded

Maintaining emotional balance is crucial for leaders to feel confident and secure during crises. Strategies like self-regulation and mindfulness help your audience feel empowered to make clear, rational decisions amid uncertainty, reinforcing their sense of control.

The practice of mindfulness, in particular, stands out for its simplicity and efficacy. By focusing on the present moment and acknowledging our emotions without judgment, we can navigate a crisis with a calm, steady hand. This grounded approach not only enhances our own decision-making but also acts as a stabilizing force for those around us, fostering a sense of security and trust.

Communicating in Crisis

Effective communication is the lifeline of crisis management. Emotional intelligence informs a communication style that can mitigate panic, clarify confusion, and inspire action. It's about tuning in to the team's emotional undercurrents, delivering messages with empathy and authenticity, and actively listening to concerns and suggestions. This empathetic approach to communication ensures that everyone feels understood and valued, fostering a sense of unity and shared purpose.

An emotionally intelligent approach to communication emphasizes transparency and reassurance, helping your audience feel valued and confident that their concerns are acknowledged and addressed, fostering collective trust and purpose.

Case Studies

Real-life examples vividly illustrate the transformative power of emotional intelligence in crises. Take, for instance, a community leader's response to a natural disaster. Leveraging EI, the leader navigated the aftermath by focusing on clear, empathetic communication and establishing a crisis response team that prioritized the emotional well-being of the community alongside physical recovery efforts. This emotionally intelligent approach fostered a sense of solidarity, resilience, and hope, inspiring the community and laying the foundation for its recovery and growth.

Another case involves a tech startup facing a critical product failure shortly before launch. The CEO, leveraging emotional intelligence, addressed the team not with blame but with empathy and resolve. By openly discussing the failure, acknowledging the team's hard work, and focusing on solutions rather than recriminations, the CEO transformed a potential morale-crushing event into a unifying challenge. The team rallied, working collaboratively to address the issues, resulting in a successful launch and a stronger, more cohesive company culture.

These case studies underscore the pivotal role of emotional intelligence in transforming crises into opportunities for leadership, team building, and personal growth. They demonstrate that, even in the face of uncertainty and disruption, EI equips us to navigate crises with compassion, clarity, and resilience.

The Global Leader: Emotional Intelligence Across Cultures

In our increasingly interconnected world, leadership involves navigating a mosaic of cultures, each defined by its unique values, norms, and ways of communication. The confluence of emotional intelligence (EI) and cultural intelligence emerges as a crucial nexus for global leaders, a meeting point where the ability to understand and manage emotions intersects with the nuanced comprehension of cultural differences. This symbiosis is not merely beneficial but vital for those at the helm of multicultural teams, where the depth of empathy and the breadth of cultural awareness can bridge worlds, fostering an environment of inclusivity and mutual respect.

The dance of cross-cultural communication, intricate and delicate, requires more than the basic steps of linguistic proficiency or surface-level understanding of cultural practices. It demands a deep, empathetic engagement with the emotional currents that flow beneath the surface of verbal and non-verbal exchanges. Emotional intelligence, in this context, serves as the compass that guides leaders through the complex emotional landscapes of diverse teams, enabling them to recognize and validate the feelings and perspectives of individuals from varied cultural backgrounds. This recognition is the first step toward transcending cultural barriers, creating a shared language of empathy that goes beyond words.

Strategically navigating these cultural differences requires a proactive approach, in which leaders not only seek to understand their team members' cultural backgrounds but also actively cultivate an environment that sees diversity as an asset rather than a challenge. This involves acknowledging and celebrating cultural differences, encouraging team members to share their unique perspectives and experiences, and integrating these insights into the team's collective problem-solving processes. Such practices not only enrich the team's creative potential but also strengthen the bonds of trust and respect that underpin effective collaboration.

Building global teams that thrive on diversity requires a foundation of emotional intelligence that is both deep and broad, capable of adapting to the fluid dynamics of cross-cultural interactions. Leaders equipped with EI are adept at creating spaces where team members feel seen, heard, and valued, irrespective of their cultural origins. This inclusivity is not a byproduct of happenstance but the result of intentional actions and policies that prioritize empathy, respect, and understanding. From the design of multicultural team-building activities to the implementation of communication protocols that respect cultural preferences and norms, every decision is infused with an awareness of the emotional and cultural dimensions of team dynamics.

The success stories of global leaders who have harnessed the power of emotional and cultural intelligence to navigate cross-cultural challenges are as diverse as the teams they lead. These narratives often share common themes of transformation and growth, illustrating how empathy and cultural awareness can turn potential conflicts into opportunities for innovation and deeper connection. One such story involves a leader who, faced with the challenge of merging teams from different cultural backgrounds, initiated a series of 'cultural exchange' workshops. These workshops provided a platform for team members to share their cultural traditions, values, and communication styles, fostering curiosity and mutual appreciation. The outcome was a team that not only worked well together but also developed innovative solutions that drew on their diverse cultural perspectives, ultimately leading to breakthroughs that would have been unimaginable in a more homogenous setting.

Another tale of cross-cultural leadership success centers on a leader who navigated the delicate process of negotiating a partnership between companies from vastly different cultural contexts. Recognizing the potential for misunderstanding and conflict, the leader employed emotional intelligence to empathize with the concerns and priorities of both parties, using this understanding to guide the negotiation process. By focusing on building emotional connections and finding common ground, the leader facilitated a partnership that respected the cultural values and business objectives of both companies, laying the groundwork for a successful, mutually beneficial collaboration.

These stories underscore the transformative potential of emotional and cultural intelligence in global leadership. They highlight that, in a world where cultural boundaries are increasingly porous, the ability to navigate them with empathy and understanding is not just a leadership skill but a necessity. For global leaders, integrating emotional and cultural intelligence is key to building teams that not only transcend cultural differences but also leverage them as a source of strength and innovation. In this way, emotional intelligence becomes the bridge that connects not only individuals and teams but also cultures and nations, fostering a global community of collaboration, understanding, and shared human experience.

The Future of Emotional Intelligence: Trends and Predictions

In today's digital era, where technology transforms every aspect of our interactions, emotional intelligence becomes crucial in navigating virtual communication and team dynamics. This shift poses unique challenges but also offers extraordinary opportunities for growth and connection. The essence of understanding and managing emotions, once confined to the realm of direct human interaction, now extends its reach into the digital domain, transforming the way we connect, collaborate, and cultivate relationships across the pixels and data streams that compose our modern world.

EI in the Digital Age

The digital age, marked by rapid technological advancements and the proliferation of remote work, demands a recalibration of the role of emotional intelligence in this new context. Virtual communication, stripped of the nuances of body language and tone, requires heightened sensitivity to the written word and an acute awareness of the emotional subtext underlying digital exchanges. Team dynamics, once fostered through face-to-face interactions, now rely on virtual platforms, challenging leaders and team members alike to forge emotional connections and foster a sense of belonging without the benefit of physical presence. In this environment, the ability to convey empathy, maintain self-awareness, and navigate team members' emotional landscapes becomes a critical skill, applying emotional intelligence principles to the subtleties of digital communication and remote collaboration.

Advancements in EI Measurement

The quest to quantify and enhance emotional intelligence has led to the integration of emerging technologies, including artificial intelligence (AI) and machine learning, into the development and measurement of EI competencies. These technologies, with their capacity to analyze vast datasets and identify patterns, offer new insights into the complex interplay of emotions and behaviors. AI-driven tools and platforms provide personalized feedback, track emotional growth, and deliver targeted strategies for enhancing specific aspects of emotional intelligence, making the development of EI skills more accessible and data-informed. As these technologies evolve, they promise to revolutionize the way we understand, measure, and cultivate emotional intelligence, offering a more nuanced and comprehensive approach to personal and professional development.

Integrating EI into Education and Training

The recognition of emotional intelligence as a critical component of success in both personal and professional realms has spurred efforts to integrate EI principles into educational curricula and professional development programs. This integration reflects a shift towards a more holistic approach to education and training, one that acknowledges the importance of emotional competencies alongside academic knowledge and technical skills. Schools, universities, and corporate training programs increasingly incorporate EI-focused modules, workshops, and assessments, equipping students and professionals with the tools they need to navigate the emotional complexities of modern life and work. This trend towards the inclusion of emotional intelligence in educational and professional development underscores a broader understanding of its role in fostering well-rounded, resilient individuals and teams.

Predictions for the Next Decade

Looking ahead, the landscape of emotional intelligence is poised for significant growth and innovation. As the digital age continues to evolve, so too will our understanding, measurement, and enhancement of EI. We can anticipate a deeper integration of emotional intelligence principles into the fabric of digital communication, with AI and machine learning playing a pivotal role in personalizing and advancing EI development. Educational and professional training programs will likely expand EI-focused content, reflecting a growing recognition of its value across various domains of life and work.

Moreover, the next decade promises a shift towards a more emotionally intelligent society, where the principles of EI are not only valued but actively cultivated across all levels of interaction. This shift has the potential to transform leadership, teamwork, and personal development, fostering environments that prioritize empathy, understanding, and emotional well-being. In this future, emotional intelligence becomes not just a skill to be developed but a foundational element of how we connect, communicate, and collaborate, shaping a world in which emotional competencies are recognized as critical for navigating the complexities of the 21st century.

In reflecting on the trajectories of emotional intelligence, from its role in the digital age to the advancements in its measurement and integration into education and training, we stand on the cusp of a new era. An era where the depth of our emotional understanding and the breadth of our emotional competencies determine the richness of our connections and the effectiveness of our collaborations. As we move forward, the principles of emotional intelligence offer a guiding light, illuminating paths to personal growth, professional success, and a more empathetic, connected society.

Chapter Summary: Emotional Intelligence Beyond Boundaries

Crisis as Opportunity

- Crises test our limits and strip away routines, exposing both vulnerabilities and strengths. Emotional intelligence (EI) provides a lens to view crises as opportunities for growth. By practicing self-awareness and empathy, leaders can turn moments of disruption into chances for team cohesion and personal development, transforming chaos into resilience.

Staying Grounded

- Self-regulation is crucial in a crisis, allowing leaders to manage emotional responses effectively. Techniques like mindfulness and breathing exercises help to stay calm, focus on the present, and make rational decisions. A grounded leader not only improves their own clarity but also serves as a stabilizing force for others, fostering trust and security within the team.

Communicating in Crisis

- Effective crisis communication is rooted in EI. Leaders should aim for transparency, empathy, and active listening to ensure information is shared accurately and to minimize panic. By acknowledging emotions, offering reassurance, and encouraging dialogue, leaders create a sense of unity, inspiring collective action and resilience.

Case Studies

- Examples from real-life crises highlight the role of EI in successful outcomes. A community leader who used empathetic communication after a natural disaster helped build resilience and unity. In another instance, a tech startup CEO navigated a product failure by focusing on team empathy and solutions, turning a potential setback into a unifying experience. These cases illustrate how EI can transform crises into powerful leadership moments.

The Global Leader: Emotional Intelligence Across Cultures

- In an interconnected world, global leaders must navigate diverse cultural landscapes. The combination of EI and cultural intelligence allows leaders to bridge cultural differences, fostering inclusion and mutual respect. By engaging empathetically with diverse perspectives, leaders can cultivate a shared understanding, laying the foundation for cross-cultural collaboration and innovation.

Building Cross-Cultural Teams

- Creating successful multicultural teams requires a commitment to celebrating diversity and understanding cultural nuances. Leaders equipped with EI can build inclusive environments where everyone feels valued. Practices such as cultural exchange workshops encourage team members to share their unique perspectives, enriching the team's creative potential and strengthening collaboration.

Success Stories

- Leaders who prioritize EI and cultural intelligence have achieved remarkable success in cross-cultural contexts. For example, a leader who merged teams from diverse backgrounds used cultural exchange workshops to foster appreciation and innovation. Another leader facilitated a complex international partnership by empathizing with both parties and ensuring a respectful, collaborative negotiation process. These stories demonstrate that EI is essential for leaders aiming to unify teams across cultural boundaries.

EI in the Digital Age

- With the rise of remote work, EI adapts to the virtual environment, where body language and tone are often absent. Leaders must rely on heightened sensitivity to digital communication cues, ensuring that empathy and understanding remain central. This adaptation of EI to the digital landscape emphasizes the importance of emotional connections in virtual team dynamics.

Advancements in EI Measurement

- Technology, including AI and machine learning, is advancing the ways we measure and develop EI. New tools can provide personalized feedback and track emotional growth, making EI development more accessible and data-driven. These innovations offer unprecedented opportunities to understand and enhance emotional intelligence in both personal and professional contexts.

Integrating EI into Education and Training

- Recognizing EI as essential to success, educational institutions and workplaces are incorporating EI into their training programs. Courses, workshops, and assessments focused on empathy, self-regulation, and social skills are becoming increasingly common, fostering resilience and adaptability among students and professionals. This trend highlights the value of EI as a critical life skill.

Predictions for the Next Decade

- The next decade will likely see further integration of EI principles into digital communication, with AI playing a role in personalizing EI development. Education and professional training will continue to expand EI-focused content, reflecting its importance across all areas of life. This trend points to a future where EI is foundational, supporting a more empathetic, connected society.

Conclusion

As emotional intelligence adapts to digital and cross-cultural contexts, it remains vital for navigating the complexities of modern life. The continued integration of EI into technology, education, and global leadership underscores its role in fostering personal growth, professional success, and a more compassionate world.

CONCLUSION
THE JOURNEY OF
EMOTIONAL INTELLIGENCE

Ah, dear reader, we've traversed the vast and vibrant landscape of emotional intelligence together, much like a grand road trip through the realms of the heart and mind. From the bustling intersections of self-awareness to the scenic routes of empathy, it's been quite the journey. Let's park our metaphorical car for a moment and reflect. At its core, this adventure was about how emotional intelligence enhances our personal and professional relationships and helps us thrive in today's whirlwind world. Amidst the chaos of deadlines and the cacophony of notifications, the quiet whispers of emotional intelligence can guide us to calmer, more meaningful interactions.

Our expedition took us through the foundational elements of emotional intelligence, starting with the basics and moving into the mastery of self-awareness and self-regulation. Recognizing these core skills can inspire confidence and a sense of purpose in your growth journey.

The transformative power of emotional intelligence is no small thing. It's about fostering resilience, enhancing empathy, improving communication, and building strong relationships. It's like discovering you've been a superhero all along, with the power to change your world from the inside out.

Reflecting on my own journey, shared in the introduction, it's clear that the road to emotional intelligence is both challenging and profoundly rewarding. From the bustling streets of Denver to the serene landscapes of Santa Fe, my path has been a testament to the growth and transformation that's possible when we commit to understanding and managing our emotions. If I could do it, navigating the complexities of life and love with a crochet hook in one hand and a suitcase in the other, so can you.

So, what's next? I urge you, dear reader, to take the wheel and drive into your own ongoing journey of emotional intelligence development. The strategies and exercises sprinkled throughout this book are your roadmap. Apply them, tweak them, make them yours, and watch as the landscapes of your relationships and workplaces transform. Remember, emotional intelligence is not a destination; it's a continuous road trip filled with learning, growth, and the occasional need for roadside assistance.

Key Takeaways for Your Road Ahead

Before you close this book, I encourage you to take a few final steps:

- **Set Daily Intentions:** Start small. Each day, set one intention related to emotional intelligence, whether it's practicing empathy, listening actively, or recognizing your emotions in the moment.
- **Reflect Regularly:** Take time to reflect on your progress. Use a journal, meditate, or sit quietly and review your actions and reactions. These moments of introspection are powerful tools for growth.
- **Embrace Lifelong Learning:** Explore further resources; books, workshops, or even mindfulness apps; that resonate with you. Remember, emotional intelligence is a continuous

journey that evolves with you, fostering hope and dedication to growth.

- **Celebrate your growth:** No matter how small. Recognizing each step forward can boost your confidence and motivate continued effort in understanding yourself and others.

Thank you, indeed, for joining me on this adventure. May the insights shared here ignite a light within you that guides you forward, illuminating paths toward deeper relationships, self-understanding, and professional fulfillment. Life is a vast tapestry, with threads of emotional intelligence woven into the fabric. Each moment is a chance to craft your masterpiece; unique, resilient, and endlessly intricate. Embrace it wholeheartedly, and let the journey enrich you and those you touch.

Here's to unlocking your full potential, transforming your world, and embracing a future filled with promise. Onward, dear reader, with heart and clarity!

With all my best,

Kimberly

APPENDIX
TOOLS, EXERCISES, AND RESOURCES

1. **Self-Reflection and Emotional Awareness**
   - **Exercise: Journaling for Self Awareness** – Reflect on daily emotional triggers and responses. Consider how to adapt journaling techniques to different emotional triggers to help readers personalize their self-awareness practices.
   - **Exercise: Emotional Compass** – Utilize visualization to navigate emotional landscapes.
   - **Mindset Check and Daily Reflections** – Set intentions in the morning and reflect on self-regulation in the evening.
2. **Building Emotional Regulation Techniques**
   - **Creating a Personal Regulation Toolkit** – Develop personalized strategies, such as cognitive reappraisal.
   - **Visualization: Calm Waters** – Technique for calming emotions through visualization. Include guidance on how readers can recognize signs of effective emotional regulation to stay motivated and track their progress.
   - **Breathing Exercises for Anxiety** – Deep breathing techniques to manage anxiety.
3. **Stress Management Strategies**

- **Stress Management Plan** – Identify key stressors, practice mindfulness, and incorporate time management techniques
- **Exercise: Mindfulness Meditation** – Engage in mindfulness to counter stress and enhance present-moment awareness

4. **Anger Management Techniques**
   - **Time-Outs and Physical Techniques** – Strategies to pause and regain control during moments of anger
   - **Channeling Anger into Advocacy** – Use anger constructively by taking positive action.

5. **Empathy and Communication Skills**
   - **Exercise: Active Listening** – Pair exercises and reflection sessions to enhance listening skills
   - **Assertiveness Training** – Techniques such as "I" statements and role-playing exercises to practice respectful self-expression

6. **Difficult Conversations**
   - **Step-by-Step Guide for Managing Tough Dialogues** – Preparation techniques and exercises for effective communication
   - **Techniques for Reflective Listening and Strategic Silence** – Enhance empathy during challenging conversations

7. **Relationship and Team Dynamics**
   - **Boundary Setting Role-Play** – Practice setting and respecting boundaries within personal and professional interactions
   - **Trust-Building Exercises** – Collaborative activities for strengthening team relationships

8. **Career Growth and Professional Development**
   - **Emotional Intelligence for Career Success** – Techniques for building empathy, stress management, and self-regulation in the workplace

- **Networking Exercises** – Strategies for emotionally intelligent networking, like active listening and feedback
9. **Continuous Learning and Self-Improvement**
   - **Exercise: Reflective Feedback Journaling** – Track responses to feedback and implement strategies for growth
   - **Visualization for Confidence** – Use visualization to overcome imposter syndrome and foster self-compassion

Each section provides readers with hands-on practices to improve emotional intelligence and overall well-being. Integrating these tools into daily routines can significantly enhance personal growth, relationship management, and professional success.

A QUICK FAVOR

If you enjoyed this book, please consider leaving an honest review where you purchased it. Your feedback helps support the author and independent publishing, and even a sentence or two can make a big difference.

Thank you for reading and supporting independent publishing. Your support means a lot and helps authors continue creating.

ABOUT KIMBERLY BURK CORDOVA

Kimberly Burk Cordova is an author, entrepreneur, and the founder of **Thrive Collective**. This platform supports creators, leaders, and entrepreneurs through publishing, leadership development, and practical tools for real-life growth. With over **30 years of experience** in leadership, technology, and business transformation, she is recognized for transforming big ideas into actionable strategies that deliver results.

Kimberly writes across topics that reflect a life fueled by curiosity: travel and culture, business and leadership, technology and modern work, food and cooking, and the everyday lessons of family life. Her wide-ranging interests invite the audience to see her as relatable and engaging.

Now based in **Santa Fe, New Mexico**, Kimberly finds inspiration in the region's art, culture, and landscapes. She shares life with her husband, Greg, and is a proud mom and grandmother to Vera and Tillman, which adds a personal touch that fosters familiarity and trust.

Connect & Explore

- **Thrive Collective** (publishing, leadership, tools): https://www.ThriveCollectiveHQ.com
- **Code Prospector** (audiobook promo codes & reviews): https://www.TheCodeProspector.com

- **Wildflower Artisans** (small-batch silver + genuine stones, curated in Santa Fe): https://wildflowerartisans.com

amazon.com/author/kimberlycordova
goodreads.com/kbcordova
youtube.com/@ThriveCollectiveHQ
facebook.com/ThriveCollectiveHQ
linkedin.com/in/kbcord
tiktok.com/@ThriveCollectiveHQ
instagram.com/thrivecollecthq
pinterest.com/ThriveCollectiveHQ
x.com/ThriveCoHQ

JOIN OUR MAILING LIST

Stay Connected with Thrive Collective

Love history, true crime, leadership insights, and travel guides? Stay in the loop with exclusive updates, behind-the-scenes content, and early access to upcoming releases from Thrive Collective. We value your interest and want you to feel part of our community.

Be the first to hear about new books, special promotions, and subscriber-only content! Your early access makes you a key part of our journey.

Join now and never miss a story, insight, or adventure. Stay connected with interests that matter to you and be part of something bigger.

https://thrivecollectivehq.com/contact

ALSO BY THRIVE COLLECTIVE

Shadows of the Past
Series: by Eliza Hawthorne

- The Vanishing Heiress
- The Music of Murder
- The Silent Witness
- Whispers from the Murder Farm
- Architect of Desire
- The Vanishing Act (Trilogy Collection)

The Growth Leader Collection:
by Kimberly Burk Cordova

- The Emotional Intelligence Advantage
- The Leadership Alchemist
- Turning Chaos into Gold
- Leadership Unlocked
- Lead Like You Mean It
- The Procrastination Cure
- Mind Games Exposed

AI & Automation Blueprint
Series: by Kimberly Burk Cordova

- Digital Mastery Guide: AI for Productivity
- Digital Mastery Guide: AI Profit Masterclass
- Digital Mastery Guide: Google Ads AI Expertise
- Digital Mastery Guide: Automation in Small Businesses
- Digital Mastery Guide: Business Systemization
- Digital Mastery Guide: AI YouTube Masterclass
- Digital Mastery Guide: Necessary Online Business Tools
- Digital Mastery Guide: Metaverse Explained

The Profitable Seller Series:
by Kimberly Burk Cordova

- FBA Freedom Formula
- Clicks That Convert
- Dropship Mastery

Profit & Protect: by
Kimberly Burk Cordova

- Create It Once, Sell It Forever
- Launch & Leverage
- Udemy Income Mastery

Empowering Small Businesses
Series: by Kimberly Burk Cordova

- The Entrepreneur's Edge
- Artificial Intelligence Unleashed
- Cybersecurity for Entrepreneurs
- Augmented and Virtual Reality

Campaigns That Convert:
by Kimberly Burk Cordova

- The SEO Blueprint
- Affiliate Mastery Blueprint

Travel Series: by Kimberly Burk Cordova

- Santa Fe Uncovered
- Santa Fe
- Denver Dossier
- Portland Your Way
- Stress Relief Travel Coloring Book For Adults

Eat Without Fear Series: by Kimberly Burk Cordova

- Eat Light, Live Bright: Low-Fat Recipes & Meal Plans

Kitchen-Table Guide from a Tech Oma: by Kimberly Burk Cordova

- Kids + AI

Content Strategy Ladder: by Kimberly Burk Cordova

- Audience X-Ray Vision

Young Legends: Inspiring True Stories of Kids' Favorite Athletes, Leaders, and Inventors

- Basketball Legends for Kids
- Soccer Legends for Kids
- Game Changers: Women Athletes
- Baseball Legends You Should Know
- The Caveman's Guide to Mental Toughness for Young Athletes

Journal Series: by Cordova Creations

- Align & Shine
- The 369 Method Manifestation
- Disconnect To Reconnect
- Simplify Your Life
- Just Write
- I Am Too Old for This Sh*t
- Dear Mom and Dad
- My Cat Rocks
- My Dog Rocks

- My Soft Girl Rocks
- My Inner Badass Rocks
- My Son Rocks
- My Daughter Rocks
- My Husband Rocks
- My Wife Rocks

BIBLIOGRAPHY

- **Adolphs, R., & Anderson, D. J.** (2018). *The Neuroscience of Emotion: A New Synthesis*. Princeton University Press.
- **American Psychological Association**. Crisis management and emotional intelligence resources. apa.org.
- **Coeckelbergh, M.** (2020). *AI Ethics*. The MIT Press.
- **Darren Menabney**. *Why Emotional Intelligence Needs Cultural Intelligence When Working Across Borders*. Forbes. Retrieved from: https://www.forbes.com/sites/darrenmenabney/2020/12/30/why-emotional-intelligence-needs-cultural-intelligence-when-working-across-borders/
- **Daniel Goleman's Emotional Intelligence Theory Explained**. Resilient Educator. Retrieved from: https://resilienteducator.com/classroom-resources/daniel-golemans-emotional-intelligence-theory-explained/
- **Emotion Regulation and Brain Plasticity**. National Center for Biotechnology Information (NCBI). Retrieved from: https://www.ncbi.nlm.nih.gov/pmc/articles/PMC3161031/
- **Emotional Triggers: What They Are and 9 Tips to Deal With Them**. BetterUp. Retrieved from: https://www.betterup.com/blog/triggers
- **Emotional Resilience: Navigating Life's Challenges with Emotional Intelligence**. Gray Group International. Retrieved from: https://www.graygroupintl.com/blog/emotional-resilience
- **Geert Hofstede's Cultural Dimensions Theory**. Cultural Intelligence insights on global leadership. Retrieved from: https://geerthofstede.com/research-and-vsm/vsm-2013/
- **Goleman, D.** (1995). *Emotional Intelligence: Why It Can Matter More Than IQ*. Bantam Books.
- **Harvard Business Review**. Building the Emotional Intelligence of Groups. Retrieved from: https://hbr.org/2001/03/building-the-emotional-intelligence-of-groups
- **Harvard Business Review**. *7 Strategies to Build a More Resilient Team*. Retrieved from: https://hbr.org/2021/01/7-strategies-to-build-a-more-resilient-team
- **Hill, R.** (2020). *9 Common Misconceptions About Emotional Intelligence*. Rachel Hill Blog. Retrieved from: https://www.rachelhill.co.nz/blog/9-misconceptions-about-eq
- **Hofstede, G.** (2001). *Culture's Consequences: Comparing Values, Behaviors, Institutions and Organizations Across Nations*. Sage Publications.

Bibliography

- **John D. Mayer & Peter Salovey**. (1997). *Emotional Intelligence as a Standard Intelligence*. Educational Psychologist.
- **Leading with Emotional Intelligence in an AI-Driven World**. Ernst & Young (EY). Retrieved from: https://www.ey.com/en_ch/workforce/leading-with-emotional-intelligence-in-an-increasingly-ai-driven-world
- **Luciana Paulise**. *9 Tactics to Master Constructive Feedback and Inspire Growth*. Forbes. Retrieved from: https://www.forbes.com/sites/lucianapaulise/2023/10/20/9-tactics-to-master-constructive-feedback-and-inspire-growth/
- **Microsoft and IBM Research Papers on AI and Emotional Intelligence**. Retrieved from: https://www.microsoft.com/research and https://www.ibm.com/research
- **NCBI**. (2021). *The Relationship between Mindfulness and Emotional Intelligence*. Retrieved from: https://www.ncbi.nlm.nih.gov/pmc/articles/PMC8161054/
- **Positive Psychology**. *13 Emotional Intelligence Activities, Exercises & PDFs*. Retrieved from: https://positivepsychology.com/emotional-intelligence-exercises/
- **Positive Psychology**. *Active Listening: The Art of Empathetic Conversation*. Retrieved from: https://positivepsychology.com/active-listening/
- **Rachel Hill**. *9 Common Misconceptions About Emotional Intelligence*. Retrieved from: https://www.rachelhill.co.nz/blog/9-misconceptions-about-eq
- **Resilient Educator**. *Daniel Goleman's Emotional Intelligence Theory Explained*. Retrieved from: https://resilienteducator.com/classroom-resources/daniel-golemans-emotional-intelligence-theory-explained/
- **The Importance Of Empathy In Leadership: How To Lead With Compassion And Understanding In 2023**. Forbes. Retrieved from: https://www.forbes.com/sites/karadennison/2023/02/24/the-importance-of-empathy-in-leadership-how-to-lead-with-compassion-and-understanding-in-2023/
- **The Relationship Between Stress, Emotional Intelligence, and Cognitive Processes**. National Center for Biotechnology Information (NCBI). Retrieved from: https://www.ncbi.nlm.nih.gov/pmc/articles/PMC6504531/
- **Verywell Mind**. *Emotional Intelligence Skills: 5 Components of EQ*. Retrieved from: https://www.verywellmind.com/components-of-emotional-intelligence-2795438
- **Webb, A.** (2019). *The Big Nine: How the Tech Titans and Their Thinking Machines Could Warp Humanity*. PublicAffairs.
- **Work–Life Balance and Mental and Physical Health Among Professionals**. NCBI. Retrieved from: https://www.ncbi.nlm.nih.gov/pmc/articles/PMC9819779/